LONGMAN PRACTICE NOTES

DEBT RECOVERY

1ST EDITION

Stephen Paul Allinson, LLB (Hons)

(Bristol), MICM, Licensed Insolvency
Practitioner
*Solicitor, Partner, CLARKE WILMOTT AND
CLARKE*

SERIES EDITOR:
CM Brand, Solicitor and Lecturer in Law
University of Liverpool

© Longman Group UK Ltd 1990

ISBN 0 85121 6935

Published by

Longman Law Tax and Finance
Longman Group UK Ltd
21/27 Lamb's Conduit Street
London WC1N 3NJ

Associated Offices:

Australia, Hong Kong, Malaysia, Singapore, USA

A CIP catalogue record for this book is available
from the British Library

Phototypeset by Input Typesetting Ltd., London
Printed in Great Britain by
Biddles Ltd, Guildford, Surrey.

ACKNOWLEDGMENTS

I would wish to express my most grateful thanks to Mrs Pamela Senabulya and Mrs Jacqueline Jones for their typing and word processing of this text; to my colleague Mark Dungworth for his invaluable help and assistance; to my wife Glenys for her proof reading and helpful practical comments, and to my children Emma and Susannah for their patience through many long hours.

The law, as I understand it, is correct as at September 1990.

CONTENTS

CONTENTS

CHAPTER 1

BASIC INFORMATION

1.1 Introduction

The recovery of money for clients has always been an important aspect of a solicitor's work. The pace of business life will continue to increase, and so clients, both personal and corporate, will require their debt to be collected quickly and efficiently to ensure their business does not suffer. In addition the solicitor's role in this field must include detailed attention to the avoidance of bad debts for clients and the setting up of efficient systems of credit control.

This book aims to provide a simple and concise procedural and practical guide to debt recovery in both the High and County Courts, with reference to the various remedies available. Emphasis is on the enforcement of a judgment rather than the procedural steps leading up to that judgment. Reference should be made (where appropriate) to the relevant Longman Practice Notes on the *County Court, High Court Procedure, Insolvency Law* and *Contentious Costs*.

1.2 Sources

A working knowledge of the following sources of reference is essential for efficient debt recovery:

- The County Court Practice ('The Green Book')
- The Supreme Court Practice ('The White Book')

1.2.1 The Green Book Published annually, this contains (amongst other things) the important Acts relating to the County Court (notably the County Courts Act 1984); the County Court Rules 1981 (Statutory Instrument (SI 1981 No 1687/L20) (as subsequently amended); County Court forms and some helpful procedural tables.

For the purposes of debt recovery the following are the most useful orders in the County Court Rules:

Order 3—Commencement of proceedings
Order 4—Venue for bringing proceedings
Order 5—Causes of action and parties

Order 6—Particulars of claim
Order 7—Service of documents
Order 9—Admission defence, counterclaim and answer
Order 16—Transfer of proceedings
Order 17—Pre-trial review
Order 25—Enforcement of judgments and orders: general
Order 26—Warrants of execution, delivery and possession
Order 27—Attachment of earnings
Order 28—Judgment summonses
Order 30—Garnishee proceedings
Order 31—Charging orders
Order 32—Receivers
Order 39—Administration orders

1.2.2 The White Book Published in two volumes, this contains in Volume 1 the Rules of the Supreme Court (brought into force by the RSC (Revision) 1965 (SI 1965 No 1776) (as amended) together with detailed notes. Volume 2 contains amongst other things High Court Forms and detailed extracts from relevant Acts.

The latest edition is The Supreme Court Practice 1991 (published in September 1990). It is soon to be published in a two-yearly cycle with biannual cumulative supplements. It was previously published in a three-yearly cycle.

For the purposes of debt recovery the most important Rules are:

Orders 5, 6, 7 & 8—Issue of proceedings
Order 10—Service of originating process
Order 12—Acknowledgment of service
Order 13—Default judgment
Order 14—Summary judgment
Order 18—Pleadings
Order 19—Default of pleadings
Order 45—Enforcement
Order 46—Writ of execution
Order 47—Writ of *Fieri Facias*
Order 48—Oral examination in the High Court
Order 49—Garnishee proceedings
Order 50—Charging orders

1.2.3 References to the County Court and High Court Rules These will be by reference to the Order and Rule numbers, eg an oral examination of a debtor in the County Court would be referred to as Ord 25, r 3 (CC) and in the High Court as Ord 48, r 1 (HC).

Care should always be taken to ensure that the most up to date edition of the White or Green Book is utilised and also a close watch should be kept on any Amendment Rules or Practice Directions in both the High and County Courts. Amendment rules are published as Statutory Instruments (as are the Rules themselves).

In particular, 1990 has seen fundamental changes in both High and County Court procedure brought about by The Rules of the Supreme Court (Amendment No 4) 1989 (SI 89/2427 (L20)) and The County Court (Amendment No 4) Rules 1989 (SI 89/2426 (L19)). Some of these came into force on 5 February 1990, others on 4 June 1990.

The key provisions of these Rules are probably more concerned with personal injury actions but are of importance for the solicitor dealing with debt recovery, for instance, it should be noted that proceedings issued after 4 June 1990 in both the High and County Courts have to be served within four months (as opposed to the previous twelve months). Six months is the period allowed if service is to be effected outside of the jurisdiction.

Furthermore, from 1 April 1990 there were important changes in the way County Court judgments are paid. These changes were brought into force by The County Court (Amendment No 3) Rules 1989 (SI 89/1838 (L17)). Whereas previously the Court accepted instalment payments prior to enforcement from the debtor, now he must make his payments direct to the creditor or his solicitor. This obviously increases the responsibility of solicitors to ensure that proper accounting methods are undertaken and accurate records kept.

More details about these changes are set out in subsequent chapters relating to enforcement.

1.3   Civil Justice Review (Cm 394)

The Lord Chancellor's Department has recently been undertaking a thorough review of all aspects of Civil Justice. This review encompasses debt recovery and therefore at the time of going to press further wide-ranging changes are anticipated. This shows that debt recovery is an ever changing subject and it is vitally important that the practitioner keeps up-to-date with any procedural changes by reference to Amendment Rules as they are published. They should always be kept with the White and Green Books.

The main thrust of the Civil Justice Review would appear to be to increase the jurisdiction of the County Court to deal with debt actions. Clause 1 of the Courts and Legal Services Bill allows the Lord Chancellor to make provisions specifying proceedings which will be commenced only in the High Court and those which will be commenced only in the County Court. It is thought that debt actions will fall into the latter category and this provision may come into force in 1991 or 1992.

1.4   Costs

The different amount of costs (often called fixed costs) that are awarded in debt actions in both the High and the County Courts are usually reviewed annually and care should always be taken to ensure that the correct costs are claimed. In general terms there are fixed costs for the standard steps in a debt recovery action (Chapter 15 sets out the most common costs and fees at the date of publication). It should be remembered that fees have to be paid to the court for most steps that are taken in an action, for example the issue of proceedings and the taking of the various enforcement steps. The fixed costs that the court awards throughout the action invariably do not equate to the true cost of the solicitor's time. With this in mind it is vital that an accurate procedure is agreed at the outset of the solicitor/client relationship for accounting purposes.

1.5   Debt collection terms

Debt recovery and debt collection has developed its own glossary of terms and reference will be made to these throughout the text but note in particular:

Letter before action   This describes the letter that clients and solicitors invariably write putting the debtor on notice that proceedings will be commenced unless payment is received within a time period or by a date specified in that letter and which by tradition is not less than seven days.

Small Claims Court   Technically there is no such thing as a Small Claims Court but clients often refer to this when considering collecting debts not exceeding £500 in the County Court. Currently any proceedings for a sum not exceeding £500 are automatically referred to arbitration which is commonly called the Small Claims Court and dealt with under an informal procedure. The general rule is that no solicitors' costs are recoverable in the arbitration procedure except the costs on the issue of the summons, and therefore for such claims a client could find it expensive to utilise a solicitor.

Terms and conditions   Clients will often refer to their 'terms and conditions' and refer you to invoices and quotations. The terms and

4

conditions printed thereon will be an attempt to protect themselves in the event of there being problems with the payment of money pursuant to a particular contract. The terms and conditions may vary in length considerably. The solicitor should ensure he has a copy of this document before advising clients on debt recovery.

Retention of title   A phrase used to describe a Clause that often appears in terms and conditions of trading. This is an attempt by clients to prevent ownership of goods that have been supplied by them passing to the debtor until payment in full has been made. The courts have usually found that the more complicated these clauses are, the less likely they are to be legally binding.

The battle of the forms   This describes colloquially the procedure whereby in most contracts both parties may seek to obtain the contract on their standard terms and conditions. The general view is that the party which fires the last shot (that is supplies the last set of terms and conditions in the contractual scenario) will ensure his terms and conditions prevail.

Bad debt   A bad debt is a non-recoverable debt. The phrase is often used by accountants who wish solicitors to advise upon whether or not certain debts should be classed as such for the purposes of annual accounts.

Normal credit period   Many businesses and professions allow a period of time (often one month) in which an account can be settled, and this is called the normal credit period.

The District or County Court Registrar   The person who will deal with all interlocutory stages in a debt recovery action and pursuant to Ord 21, r 5 (CC), he may also deal with final hearings in the County Court. He is a senior lawyer who in essence acts as an assistant Judge. He is called the District Registrar in the High Court and the Registrar in the County Court.

County Court Bailiff   The officer of the court charged by the County Court Registrar to execute warrants of execution for creditors, which is the procedure whereby he seeks to seize goods of the debtor and sell the same to settle the debt.

High Court Sheriff   The officer of the court who carries out similar functions to the Bailiff of the County Court under High Court procedure.

Conduct money   A phrase used to describe the sum of money paid or tendered to a debtor being a reasonable sum for his travelling expenses to attend court. Such money is sometimes a prerequisite to the carrying out of certain enforcement steps (as will be seen in subsequent chapters) eg, on an adjourned hearing of an Oral Examination or Judgment Summons.

CHAPTER 2

AVOIDING BAD DEBTS

2.1 Knowing your client

The most efficient system of debt recovery is obviously to ensure that debts do not arise. Effective steps should therefore be taken at the outset by the clients and their solicitor to prevent debt problems.

2.2 Preventative advice to the client

When undertaking a new contractual relationship the client should be in a position to assess the risks of contracting and have some background knowledge of the person with whom he wishes to deal. The use of a standard proforma by clients requiring personal or company details has considerable advantages and some of that information can be used later if problems develop and the solicitor is asked to advise.

2.2.1 Bank references Bank references are often utilised but their effectiveness is perhaps questionable. The information given is usually limited. It is often more important to analyse what is not stated than what is.

2.2.2 Trade references A trade reference may be of more use, particularly if the client is himself a trader or has contacts in that field. Care should be taken, however, to check the authenticity of such references if they come from an unknown source.

2.2.3 Credit references It may be worthwhile to consider using a Credit Reference Agency. For a prescribed fee such an agency would supply known information on the credit worthiness of a debtor, eg details of any County Court judgments or other matters which are revealed concerning the debtor. If dealing with a company, the credit reference agency would often combine this information with a full company search. Care should be taken to ensure that more money is not expended than is necessary in obtaining this information as credit reference and company search information can often be duplicated.

2.2.4   Register of County Court judgments   Remember that it is only County Court (surprisingly not High Court) judgments that are registered. There has been a change from 1 April 1990 and now all County Court judgments are registered on judgment, with the exception of genuine defended cases where the losing party does not request an instalment order.

This Register is kept pursuant to the County Courts Act 1984, s 73A and is under the control of Registry Trust Limited, 173–175 Cleveland Street, London, W1P 5PE (telephone: 071 380 0133).

Upon payment of £2 per named person of a specified address, to the above organisation and completion of the form that is supplied by them, the Register will be searched and the amount of judgment, date of judgment and Court and Plaint number of any judgment revealed will be supplied. Such judgment details remain registered for a period of six years.

Copies of the form can be obtained by telephoning the company.

For full details of the new registration procedures from 1 April, reference should be made to the Register of County Court Judgments (Amendment) Regulations 1990 (SI 1990 No 491 (L3)), which includes details of the cancellation procedure when payment has been made.

Alternatively, credit agencies will often provide this service as part of their standard charges (possibly at a more expensive rate, although speed of response could be quicker). It is not possible to undertake telephone searches of the Register of County Court judgments.

2.2.5   Company searches   When dealing with a company, a search of the Company Register through reputable company agents is almost a prerequisite of contracting or otherwise dealing. A fee of approximately £25 is normally incurred but this could be money well spent. A lower charge is made for supply of company microfiches. Alternatively a personal visit to Companies House would obtain the same information. It is situate at Crown Way, Cardiff.

A full company search should reveal details of the registered office of the company; the directors, secretary and shareholdings; details of any charges or debentures and a full copy of the latest filed accounts.

Points to watch out for in company accounts
- Have they been filed? The Companies Act of 1985 provides strict filing requirements for the filing of accounts at Companies House (in general terms ten months from the relevant year end). If up-to-date accounts have not been filed ascertain the reason for this.

- What do the profit and loss accounts and balance sheet show and are these better figures than the previous years?
- Have there been recent changes of directors? If so try and ascertain the reason why.
- If bank debentures or charges are revealed, how recently were these taken? Obviously the larger the debt the more important this information becomes.

2.2.6 Terms and conditions of trading Although lawyers make much of this subject many clients do not utilise effective terms and conditions of trading. Common pitfalls include:

- A failure to incorporate the terms and conditions at the outset of trading.
- A failure to deal adequately with the other side's terms and conditions ('the battle of the forms').
- A failure to cover necessary eventualities.

(a) *Effective incorporation of terms and conditions* It is not enough simply to reveal terms and conditions of trading at the delivery of the goods stage, nor on any invoice that is appended. It may not be sufficient to have the copy of the terms and conditions available at the place where the contract is concluded unless specific attention is brought to the same. For the avoidance of doubt, the best solution is for a copy of the terms and conditions to be produced to the other side prior to the contract and for a signature to be obtained agreeing that goods will be supplied on those terms and conditions.

(b) *The battle of the forms* This doctrine means in essence that the party that delivers the last form with terms and conditions will, in the vast majority of cases, ensure that its terms and conditions are the relevant ones for the contract. Ensure therefore that the client's terms and conditions are the final document.

(c) *Establish a course of dealing* Even if your client has not delivered on each occasion his terms and conditions, if a customer has been dealt with regularly then providing the terms and conditions were brought to his attention at the outset of the trading relationship (or even at a later stage) it may be possible to establish to the court's satisfaction a course of dealing and the incorporation of your client's terms and conditions. This doctrine is, however, fraught with uncertainty and the better policy is to ensure that all terms and conditions are set out at the beginning of contract negotiations, and indeed subsequently where relevant. Remember as well, that although it perhaps does no harm to include the terms and conditions on a quotation, one interpretation of contractual negotiations could be that a quotation is simply an invitation to treat rather than an offer and is accordingly a pre-contract document.

(d)   *Effective terms and conditions*   Any work of this nature cannot possibly deal with the myriad of terms and conditions that could be entered into in any contractual relationship. Certain examples, however, of some important terms and conditions are set out below:

- Price and payment clauses—make provision for increase if possible, with a price variation clause.
- Interest—provide for payment of contractual interest in default of payment of an account within a specified period.
- Specified credit terms—eg 28 days before interest becomes payable.
- Reservation of title clause—this is a most complicated area of law, but in essence it is an attempt by a seller to say that buyers do not own the goods until payment in full has been made and if payment in full is not made, the seller is entitled to recover the goods. This may sound satisfactory in theory, but in practice there are a number of problems. Consider for example, if the goods then become mixed with other goods, or involved in a manufacturing process, or indeed if the goods are then passed to a third party. Because of this, there have been a number of attempts to create wide and complicated reservation of title clauses which, in general terms, have not found favour with the courts. The most recent case was *Tatung (UK) Ltd* v *Galex Telesure Ltd and Others* (1989) 5 BCC 325, which reiterated the theory that many of these retention of title clauses created a charge in favour of the supplier and therefore must be registered pursuant to s 395 of the Companies Act 1985. If such a charge was not registered the clause (regardless of other arguments) would be unenforceable in any event.

    Accordingly, caution must be undertaken when advising or drafting retention of title clauses. These clauses become particularly important when dealing with a receiver or liquidator after the company has found itself in difficulties and formal insolvency proceedings are following.
- International contracts—with businesses now becoming more international it is not unusual for dealings to be with companies or individuals in other countries. To that end, ensure that there is an effective choice of law term in the contract which provides that in the event of a dispute then the relevant law will be that of the country in which the client is based (normally of course English Law), and that the Courts of that country will have jurisdiction.

2.2.7 Personal guarantees from directors If dealing with a company for the first time or the history of that company is not promising, consider obtaining a personal guarantee from the directors (or possibly a cross guarantee from another company, perhaps in the same group).

The desire or otherwise of the directors to give such a guarantee may be indicative of the status of the company. The type and form of such guarantee will inevitably vary and if it is too strict it may have an adverse effect and the customer may not wish to deal on those terms. Alternatively, if drafted in a general way it may not protect the client in every circumstance which later occurs. At the end of the day a commercial decision must be taken by the client with his solicitor as to how detailed such a clause should be.

CHAPTER 3

COMMENCEMENT OF PROCEEDINGS

3.1 Taking instructions

It is generally only when earlier steps have failed that clients turn to solicitors for the collection of outstanding debts. At this stage it is vital that solicitors act promptly, efficiently and correctly. It is also at this stage that the importance of a client questionnaire is seen. In addition, the better the procedures that have been adopted by the client the more chance there is of a successful recovery. The background as to the collection of the debt may vary as will the amount involved but the procedures are similar. At the first appointment ensure the client brings in all necessary paper work in connection with the debt in particular:

- The invoice document upon which the debt is based.
- Any terms and conditions of trading which it is alleged became incorporated into the contract.
- Any pre-contract correspondence.
- Correspondence between the client and the debtor post-contract.
- Any up-to-date ledger account showing any monies received.

With this information before you, the obtaining of the initial instructions becomes easier and at the first interview a checklist for initial instructions should be completed.

3.1.1 Standard pro forma for use by solicitor An example of the type of relevant information that a solicitor will require when acting for a client in debt recovery, which should be obtained at the first meeting, is set out below.

Although each case will clearly vary considerably a solicitor should ensure that as many of the following points as possible are obtained at the initial interview.

Section A—Client
- Name.
- Address (or registered office if company).
- Particulars of trade or business contact person (credit manager, director etc).

- Contact telephone number and/or fax number.

Section B—Details of debtor and debt
- Name of debtor—individual or company.
- Address, registered office.
- Trade name.
- Bank account details.
- Partnership—full names of the partners and private addresses.
- Company—full names and addresses of all directors.
- Details of how debt arose (copies of the invoices etc; dates of any payments made).
- Copies of any correspondence received or sent by client in relation thereto.
- Indication by client of possible dispute which may form a Defence-/Counterclaim.

Section C—Terms and conditions of trading
- Production of terms and conditions of trading by client.
- Details of credit period allowed (7, 14 or 30 days or end of month following invoice date).
- Is contractual interest claimed by client—if so, at what rate?
- Is there a retention of title clause? If so is it likely to be effective?
- Were any terms and conditions supplied by the debtor? (If so, obtain a copy and ascertain when it was supplied).
- The battle of the forms—who fired the last shot? When was it fired?

Section D—Miscellaneous
- Have any payments been made—if so, when and how were they credited? If by cheque, obtain the bank details.
- Has any other person guaranteed the debts of the debtor to the client?
- Any information known concerning the financial security of the defendant, eg is any property owned upon which security could be taken?
- Has a company search been undertaken or credit check made.
- Are there any known assets of value?

Section E—The continuation of the action
- How often should reports be made to the client—weekly, monthly or otherwise?
- Is the client prepared to proceed to formal insolvency procedure if necessary?
- What costs limit has been placed on action by the client before review?

3.1.2 Further useful information It may be necessary at this point to undertake some of the searches described in section 2.2 if these have not been undertaken by the client at an early stage.

Perhaps the best information can be obtained from the client himself. Alternatively, a knowledgeable and well informed enquiry agent may well be able to provide certain information at reasonable cost. Instructions should always be sought from the client as to how far this pre-action process should be taken. If very little is known about the debtor however, then it may be sensible, and result in a saving of money in the long run.

3.1.3 Other searches and registers

- Land Charges Registry. A search against the debtor's name at this registry may reveal second or third mortgages (as these have to be registered) and may therefore supply useful information as to whether a charging order should be contemplated. In addition they may reveal whether there are previous charging orders or alternatively whether there are bankruptcy proceedings pending or a Bankruptcy Order made. The cost is £1.00 per name. The address of the Land Charges Registry is Search Section, Burrington Way, Plymouth, PL5. If this search is undertaken it is important that the debtor's full names are known.

- Land Registry. If the title is registered then a parcel index map search can be made to confirm this and discover the title number. However, no copies of entries on the register can be obtained without either the consent of the registered proprietor of the land or his solicitor unless the registrar grants an order upon an application for a charging order. The cost of a Parcel Index Map Search is £6.00. Changes are proposed for the end of 1990 to make the title available to public inspection.

- Attachment of earnings index—pursuant to Order 27, r2 (CC). The proper officer of every court keeps a nominal index of the debtors residing within the district of his court in respect of whom there are in force attachment of earnings orders which have been made by that court or of which the Proper Officer has received notice from another court. This index can be searched by any person having a judgment or order against a person believed to be residing within the district of the court and a certificate will be issued. If an attachment of earnings order is revealed then consideration should be given to consolidating with this (see section **10.4**).

  The standard form is Form N 336 in the County Court forms.

- Register of Bills of Sale. This is a more specialised register. To be effective all bills of sale must be registered at the Filing

Department, Central Office, Royal Courts of Justice and if there is concern that certain assets may be subject to a bill of sale, a search should be done there. The fee for an official certificate of the result of a search in one name in any register or index number under the custody of the registrar of bills of sale is £2 and for every additional name, if included in the same Certificate, an extra fee of £1.

- Insolvency. An up-to-date confirmation of whether or not a winding-up petition has been presented against a company can be obtained by telephoning the Companies Court (which keeps a central index of winding-up petitions) on 071 936 6329. This is of particular importance in contemplating winding-up proceedings to check whether or not a petition is in force and would provide more up-to-date information than the company search.

For individuals there is a register of bankruptcy notices and petitions kept at Thomas More Building, Carey Street, London, but as stated above a search at the Land Charges Registry will reveal whether there is a pending bankruptcy or if the Bankruptcy Order has been made.

3.2 The letter before action

Most solicitors will wish to write a letter before action before proceeding to the court process. It is not wrong to issue proceedings immediately, but there is a risk that a Registrar, upon hearing the matter and being told by the debtor that a letter before action has not been written, may disallow the interest or the costs which would normally be awarded. For this reason a solicitor's letter is often written. One way to avoid this would be for the clients to have written a suitable letter before action, indicating that in default of hearing within a requisite time period (which should give a sufficient period for response and this is usually seven days) then matters will be placed in the hands of a solicitor and interest and costs will be added. Most solicitors however, prefer that this letter is drafted themselves and a suggested precedent is set out below.

3.2.1 Sample letter before action

Dear Sirs,

Re: (*name of client*)

We represent (*name of client*) of (*address of client*) and have been instructed concerning the sum of £(*amount of debt*) that is outstanding and overdue for payment from yourselves.

We must advise you that unless we receive your remittance or acceptable proposals for payment within the next seven days from the date of this letter we are instructed to issue Court proceedings.

If this is necessary no doubt you will appreciate this could well result in the amount to be paid by you being increased with the fees, costs and interest that will be claimed therein in addition to the debt.

We are authorised to accept payment from henceforth on behalf of our clients. Your payment should therefore be made payable to this firm at this office and be accompanied by a stamped, addressed envelope if a receipt is required.

We would advise against making payment by post in cash but if you choose to do so that will be at your risk.

Yours faithfully,

3.2.2 Points to note in the letter before action Ensure the letter is properly and correctly addressed. If pursuing a company, mark it for the attention of the director (and name him or her if possible). There is a risk however in doing this if the director is away from the office and he is later able to show that it did not come to his attention within the stated time period. In this case any future action could be delayed. If pursuing an individual, then again ensure the correct full name and address is utilised. If there is some doubt about these, basic checks either in the telephone directory or possibly with the Electoral Registration Office may elicit some information.

If pursuing a partnership it is always better to sue the individuals rather than relying only on the trade name of the partnership because of the more effective enforcement action that is available. This is another reason for ensuring that clients obtain the full names of all the partners. In this case, the letter before action should be addressed to the individuals quoting the partnership name, eg John Smith and Hubert Brown, Smith & Brown Painters and Decorators.

State clearly the name and address of your client and the amount of the debt. Often invoice details are quoted, but this practice becomes complicated if the debt is made up of a number of invoices.

Make it clear that in default of payment within a requisite time period (normally seven, ten or fourteen days) proceedings will follow without further notice and will include claims for interest and costs.

Make it clear to where payment should be directed. This is particularly important in the light of the recent decision of the Court of Appeal in *Anglian Water Authority* v *Wilson* (1989) *The Times*

30 August 1989. In that case the Court of Appeal held that because the plaintiff water authority had decreed that payment for water charges could be made at any branch of a number of designated banks, at a Post Office or by giro transfer, or by post to a particular box number then the cause of action arose because of the failure to pay at any one of these points. As a result of this it was open to the plaintiff water authority to issue proceedings within the relevant County Court for any of the above places of payment.

Although this case may be open to interpretation, it is therefore submitted that if the letter before action stresses that payment should be made at the solicitor's office then even if the cause of action did not arise within the plaintiff solicitor's County Court district, that particular County Court should accept a summons from the plaintiff's solicitors because the jurisdiction would be established by the place of payment being indicated in the letter before action.

It should perhaps be stressed that it would still be open for a defendant to apply for a transfer later on in the proceedings (Ord 16, r 4(2) (CC)). A similar power exists for the judge or registrar to transfer matters of his own motion (Ord 16, r 4(1) (CC)).

3.3   High Court or County Court?

3.3.1   Technical jurisdiction   The County Court only has jurisdiction in debt matters (which are contract matters) where sums of up to £5,000 are involved, (see s 15 of the County Courts Act 1984 for general jurisdiction details). Therefore, if a greater sum is to be sued for, the High Court must be utilised unless the parties consent to the County Court having jurisdiction for a sum greater than £5,000 (County Courts Act 1984, s 18). Note, however, that the County Court also has other specific jurisdiction in specialised actions and of particular concern for the practitioner in the debt field is its increased jurisdiction for the recovery of goods in hire purchase, conditional sale agreements and agreements under the Consumer Credit Act of 1974. For agreements made after 18 May 1985, it has jurisdiction for the recovery of goods providing the sum does not exceed £15,000 and where the hirer or buyer is not a body corporate and where one-third of the price has been paid.

Accordingly, if a Consumer Credit Act claim is brought in the County Court, check carefully whether the High or County Court should be utilised and also ensure the provisions of the Consumer Credit Act 1974 have been complied with.

3.3.2   Advantages of the High Court   Although the County

Court has technical jurisdiction in most cases for sums up to and including £5,000 there is still the option of proceeding in the High Court. Practitioners often identify advantages for choosing the High Court. In particular, note:

- the more efficient enforcement procedures available in the High Court;
- service is effected, and therefore controlled, by the creditor or his representatives rather than by the Court staff as is normal for the County Court;
- interest runs after judgment on a High Court judgment (but not on a County Court judgment);
- there are not the same jurisdictional problems for issuing within the High Court as in the County Court. It is possible to elect to issue in a District Registry of your choice but at the risk of the defendant applying to transfer to another District Registry which is more convenient to him.

Having made the above points however, there may be cost penalties if proceedings are taken in the High Court and low sums awarded. If under £600 is awarded on a default judgment in the High Court, then no costs are allowed (and similar considerations apply for a summary judgment application).

For this reason, practitioners would not issue proceedings for sums less than £600 in the High Court, but certainly serious consideration should be made for the utilisation of the High Court for sums approaching £1,000 or more.

3.3.3 Advantages of the County Court In the light of the above, it is probably thought that there are few advantages to utilising the County Court, although it should be stressed that the practices of County Courts vary and if the particular County Court for your district is one with whom a good relationship is enjoyed then this may be an advantage in itself.

Other advantages are:

- the costs of issue in the County Court are less than in the High Court;
- there is the procedure for registering a County Court judgment (which does not exist in the High Court), and this can prompt payment as it can affect the debtor's credit worthiness;
- no attachment of earnings orders are available in the High Court (except for rare cases);
- a simpler and cheaper process of oral examination of a debtor exists in the County Court;

- a simpler and cheaper process exists for a warrant of execution compared with a writ of *fieri facias* in the High Court;
- Administration orders exist in the County Court (see section 11.5).

Against these advantages should be weighed the fact that no interest is payable on a County Court judgment and also because the County Court system is 'court centred' all orders are drawn by the court which may mean there is a delay before they are received by solicitors.

3.3.4 Transfer from the High to the County Court

3.3.4 Transfer from the High to the County Court Pursuant to the County Courts Act 1984, s 40 there are considerable powers to transfer from the High Court to the County Court. Indeed, the majority of defended debt actions commenced in the High Court are transferred at a later stage to the County Court. The Court may do this at any stage of the proceedings and would either do it of its own motion, or upon an application of one of the parties.

The criteria to be satisfied are:

- that the parties consent to a transfer, or
- that the sum is within the County Court's jurisdiction, or
- no important question of law or fact is involved.

In debt actions, the transfer to a County Court would normally be undertaken when a matter becomes defended either upon an application of one party, or alternatively at the summons for directions stage, or possibly if an application for Summary Judgment pursuant to Order 14 (HC) is unsuccessful.

There is also provision in the County Courts Act 1984, ss 41 and 42 for a transfer of County Court proceedings to the High Court, but it is rarely utilised in debt actions. Practitioners should note that there is a strong move to bring all debt matters into the County Court system and certainly for sums where less than £25,000 is at issue. Practice directions issued in 1988 have made it quite clear that the Masters and District Registrars will be transferring actions more readily. For further details of these statements see the Practice Directions set out in [1988] 2 All ER 64 and [1988] 3 All ER 95.

3.4 Interest

Reference has already been made to the importance of interest in debt proceedings. Indeed the correct claiming of interest can result in considerable compensation for the client and it is incumbent upon practitioners to ensure that the principles and rules are correctly followed.

3.4.1 Preliminary points   In considering whether a debt comes within the County Court limit (£5,000) the question of interest pursuant to s 69 of the County Courts Act 1984 is ignored. However if interest is claimed pursuant to the original contractual arrangement this is taken into account. The current rate of interest pursuant to the Judgment Debts (Rate of Interest) Order 1985 is 15 per cent.

Remember that your client's terms and conditions will normally allow for either seven days or twenty-eight days or one month for payment and therefore the interest calculation should be made from that date and not the date of invoice, unless the terms and conditions declare otherwise.

If the client's terms and conditions include contractual interest then any writ or summons must refer and plead to that, although it may be advisable to plead the statutory interest in the alternative form. Statutory interest in the High Court is based on s 35A of the Supreme Court Act 1981. Statutory interest in the County Court is based on s 69 of the County Courts Act 1984.

3.4.2 Rules for pleading interest in a debt action   In order to ensure recovery in both the High Court and County Court, interest must be pleaded specifically: the amount of interest claimed must be shown and the rate at which, and the period for which, it is claimed. Failure to do this could mean that the Court would disallow interest. Although it is always possible to apply at any date to amend the interest claimed, there could be penalisation in costs. Correct pleading will show the amount of interest claimed, the number of days upon which it is claimed and the rate of interest up to the date of issue of proceedings, and thereafter it will plead a daily rate of interest from the date of issue of proceedings until judgment or sooner payment.

3.4.3 An example of the interest pleading on a Statement of Claim   The following is an example of the prayer to a statement of claim. The general view is that it is not necessary to claim interest in the body of the statement of claim but the prayer should be carefully drafted as set out below (assuming for the purposes of this example that there is only one invoice and thus one interest calculation):

AND

the Plaintiff claims:

(1)   the sum of (debt amount)

(2)   ... interest on the sum claimed in paragraph (1) above pursuant to s 35A of the Supreme Court Act 1981 at the rate of 15 per cent per annum from the (date from which interest is claimed) to the date hereof being ... days.

(3)   Interest on the sum claimed in paragraph (1) hereof pursuant to s 35A of the Supreme Court Act 1981 at the rate of 15 per cent per annum from the date hereof to the date of judgment or sooner payment which is a daily rate of ...

(4)   Alternatively interest claimed pursuant to s 35A, Supreme Court Act 1981 on the amount claimed in paragraph (1) hereof at such rate and for such period as the Court may deem just.

The final clause is put in to cover the situation of there being an error in the interest calculation.

3.4.4   An example of the interest pleading in a Particulars of Claim pursuant to s 69 of the County Courts Act 1984

Again this should be set out in the prayer for relief after the Particulars of Claim and should read as follows (again assuming one invoice and one interest calculation):

AND

the plaintiff claims:

(1)   the sum of (debt amount)

(2)   ... interest on the sum claimed in paragraph (1) above pursuant to s 69 of the County Courts Act 1984 at the rate of 15 per cent per annum from the (date from which interest is claimed), to the date hereof being ... days.

(3)   Interest on the sum claimed in paragraph (1) hereof pursuant to s 69 of the County Courts Act 1984 at the rate of 15 per cent per annum from the date hereof to the date of judgment or sooner payment which is a daily rate of ...

(4)   Alternatively interest pursuant to s 69 of the County Courts Act 1984 on the amount claimed in paragraph (1) hereof at such rate and for such period as the court may deem just.

3.4.5   Costs

Both the High Court and County Court lay down fixed costs upon the issue of proceedings in terms of costs to be paid and recoverable costs. In the High Court there is a fixed fee for the

20

issue of a writ (currently £70), whereas in the County Court the fees vary depending on the amount for which proceedings are issued. Any sum over £500 however has a fixed fee of £43.

Reference should be made to the current fees orders of both the High and County Courts (see Chapter 15). Set fees and different costs figures are also awarded in both the High and County Courts, depending on the mode of service utilised. The most common fees for debt recovery, correct as at the date of publication but reviewed each year, are set out in Chapter 15.

3.5   The correct defendant

Again, the importance of full information to establish the identity of the correct defendant becomes relevant here and the importance of the client questionnaire referred to earlier cannot be overstressed. The three most common situations in debt recovery are clearly the pursuing of an individual, a partnership or a company.

3.5.1   The individual defendant   Providing the correct full name and current address is known there are no special rules to follow. If the debt is a joint and several one (for example a joint bank account for a husband and wife) then both should be named as defendants.

3.5.2   A partnership   Ensure first of all that your client is sure he is dealing with a partnership and not a limited company. Reference should be made to Ord 81 (HC) and Ord 5, r 9 (CC). The advantage of suing the partners as individuals, rather than solely in the firm's name is that if a judgment is obtained against a partnership name then leave must subsequently be obtained to enforce against the assets of the individual partners. In certain cases it may be difficult, of course, to find the identity of the individual or individuals, but assistance may be obtained from the Business Names Act 1985. This provides a requirement for disclosure of names of partners and, in relation to each person so named, an address in Great Britain at which service of any document relating in any way to the business will be effective. These names must be stated on all business letters, written orders for goods or services to be supplied to the business, invoices and receipts issued in the course of the business and written demands for the payments of debts arising in the course of the business. In addition, at any premises where the business is carried on, there must be displayed in a prominent position a notice containing such names and addresses.

There was previously a Registry of Business Names, but that is no longer operative.

Furthermore, once proceedings have been issued a plaintiff is able to make a formal demand, if proceedings have been issued against a partnership, for the names of the individual partners and their places of residence. This request must be complied with by the partnership and all names and addresses must be given of those who were partners in the firm when the cause of action arose (see Ord 81, r 1 (HC) and Ord 5, r 9(2) (CC)).

3.5.3 The corporate defendant The full and correct name and the current registered office of a company will have been obtained from a search at Companies House (the details revealed by this procedure have been referred to in Chapter 2) but it is always advisable just before issuing proceedings to check that the company has not been wound up or is not subject to any form of insolvency process. Any company agents should be able to tell you that information, or alternatively, enquiries can be made, as previously stated, at Companies House or at the Companies Court. It is clearly frustrating both for a solicitor and his client to issue proceedings and then to find that a company has already been put into liquidation. It should of course be remembered that the liquidation of a company effectively stays the legal process that is being pursued.

3.6   Issue of proceedings

3.6.1 General points Reference has already been made to the choice between High and County Court for the issue of process and the advantages and disadvantages connected with the same. In the High Court, debt actions will be commenced in the Queen's Bench Division, either at the Central Office in London or in the District Registries. There is no requirement to issue the process where the cause of action occurred, or indeed where the defendant resides. However, care must be taken if process is being undertaken in a District Registry where the defendant does not reside or where the cause of action did not arise to cross out the relevant section on the reverse of a writ.

In the County Court, process must be issued either in the Court where the defendant resides or alternatively where the cause of action arose. To this end, the importance of persuading the Court that the cause of action arose in the plaintiff's home Court, pursuant to *Anglian Water Authority* v *Wilson (supra)* is firmly established.

In the High Court, if the writ is issued out of a District Registry and the plaintiff has not endorsed that the cause of action arose in that District Registry, then the defendant can apply for a transfer of the action by completing paragraph 4 of the Acknowledgment of Service and, if the plaintiff does not object to this transfer within eight days, then the proceedings will automatically be transferred as requested by the defendant. If there is an objection then there will then be an interlocutory hearing before the Registrar. At that hearing he will consider the balance of convenience between the parties, and recent unreported cases that are referred to in the White Book indicate that the balance of convenience will normally be at the Court in which the plaintiff's solicitors reside as they would have conduct of most interlocutory applications.

3.6.2 High Court issue procedure The original writ should be completed and taken together with two copies (plus one extra copy for every additional defendant) and a fee of £70 to the appropriate District Registry or Central Office. The writ will be checked and one copy retained by the court, one marked as the original which will be retained by the plaintiff's solicitor and the service copy or copies returned.

In the vast majority of debt cases the statement of claim will be endorsed on the writ rather than being served separately, and law stationers provide appropriate forms of writ for this purpose. The pleading for a debt case will be relatively simple and will generally refer to the invoice for which payment has not been made or alternatively the cheque which has been dishonoured, or the services that have been rendered but have not been paid for. Thereafter interest is pleaded as set out earlier in this chapter.

Remember that a statement of claim should be signed by the solicitors if they have drafted the same. In addition the court's copy will also have to be signed in the left hand margin by the individual issuing the proceedings.

3.6.3 County Court issue procedure In debt matters the Default Summons is utilised in the County Court system. The Particulars of Claim set out therein are akin to a statement of claim with the appropriate interest pleading.

The plaintiff's solicitor should complete a request for the issue of a Default Summons (form N 201) and in simple debt cases the Particulars of Claim can be endorsed thereon. These should then be taken together with a copy for each defendant to the appropriate County Court together with the issue fee (see Chapter 15) and proceedings will be issued and a plaint note quoting the action number forwarded to the plaintiff. The plaint note will include the date of service to enable calculations to be undertaken by the plaintiff for the entry of a judgment in default. A plaintiff can apply for judgment on the fifteenth day after the date of service.

It should be noted that plaintiffs' solicitors undertaking a lot of debt work, can now prepare their own summonses on form N 1 rather than the request form and furthermore, a streamlined procedure has been commenced in 1990 for plaintiffs' solicitors who undertake bulk issue to do this through a bulk issue centre based in Lichfield. For further information about this procedure solicitors should contact the Bulk Issue Liaison Officer at the Lord Chancellor's Department, c/o Lichfield County Court, Beaconsfield House, Sandford Street, Lichfield, Staffs, WS13 6QA; telephone 0543 414178. In normal circumstances the Court will append a form of Admission Defence and Counterclaim to the summons and serve the defendant direct, although again, a request can be made for the plaintiff's solicitors to undertake service themselves.

3.7   Service of proceedings

There are the following possibilities of service of proceedings:

- service on solicitor authorised by the defendant;
- postal service (first class post);
- 'Letter box' service (individuals only);
- County Court—service by Court bailiff;
- substituted service.

In the High Court, service by whatever method is effected by the solicitors or clients themselves or alternatively by enquiry agents, or authorised process servers.

Postal service is still the method that is utilised more than any other method. Remember that service is by first class post and *not* recorded delivery as this is precluded by the rules. Service by post however, is fraught with uncertainty and professional debtors may be able to promote appropriate delays by claiming never to have received summonses or writs.

For this reason personal or 'letter box' service is an attractive option and promotes certainty.

Substituted service should only be necessary where it is clear that the defendant is evading service. However, the procedure to be adopted for an order for substituted service is cumbersome and will inevitably promote delays (see Ord 65, r 4 (HC) and Ord 7, r 8 (CC)).

If solicitors have been acting for the defendant then service can be effected with their agreement on those solicitors and in this case the original writ together with the service copy should be sent and the original will then be endorsed by the defendant's solicitor acknowledging service. This procedure is set out in Ord 10, r 1 (4) (HC). In the County Court the comparable rule is Ord 7, r 11 (CC) and the solicitor there gives a certificate of his acceptance of service, instead of endorsing a memorandum on a copy of the summons.

3.7.1   Computation of time before service of proceedings   The date of service is computed as follows:

- Personal service—the date of actual service.
- Postal or letterbox service of a High Court writ on an individual or firm—the seventh day after the date of posting or insertion.
- Postal service of a High Court writ on a limited company—the second working day after the date of posting if first class post is used, or the fourth day after posting if second-class post is used.
- Postal service of the default summons by a County Court upon an individual or firm—seventh day after the date of posting as evidenced by the plaint note forwarded to the plaintiff's solicitor by the County Court staff.
- Postal service of the default summons by a County Court upon a company—second day after posting (first class) as evidenced by the plaint note forwarded to plaintiff's solicitor.
- Service on solicitor authorised by the defendant—effective on the date upon which the solicitor endorses his acceptance of service on the original writ or summons or completes a certificate of service.

3.7.2   Where should service be effected?
(a) Partnership   If, as is desired, the partnership is sued in the individual's names then service is effected in a normal manner upon the individuals. If however, the partnership is named as the defendant then service can be effected upon any partner personally or alternatively at the principal place of business of the firm by leaving the summons with any person appearing to have control or management of the firm. However, this is only if a partnership is still in existence (see Ord 81, r 3 (HC) and Ord 7, r 13 (CC)).
(b) Service on a company   In the High Court a company must be served at its registered office either by leaving or sending a writ. In the County Court there has been an interesting change in the rules from 18 July 1989 with the substitution of a new Ord 7, r 14 (CC). This permits service at either the company's registered office or at any place of business of the company which has some real

connection with the cause or matter in issue. However, although this may work to the advantage of the plaintiffs' solicitors, specific provision is made for setting aside when it appears the summons did not come to the knowledge of 'an appropriate person' in due time. 'An appropriate person' is not defined and if this method is utilised, practitioners may find that they are faced with more applications to set aside and the Registrar may be bound to accept the same if a reasonable excuse is offered by the defendant company's representatives.

3.8 What if the defendant resides out of the jurisdiction?

In the High Court, service out of the jurisdiction is set out in Ord 11 (HC) and in the County Court in Ord 8 (CC). However, the Civil Jurisdiction and Judgments Act 1982 has certainly made it easier for proceedings to be commenced and continued against defendants domiciled outside England and Wales. Detailed reference to the orders should be made to see whether or not service with or without leave can be effected in the country in which the defendant is domiciled.

CHAPTER 4

THE CONTINUATION
OF AN ACTION

The purpose of this chapter is to indicate how effective and swift action with the relevant Rules of Court in both the High and County Courts can ensure that a successful recovery is obtained for clients. Other Practice Notes in this series (in particular *High Court Procedure* and *County Court*) deal with the progress of a defended action. Inevitably the vast majority of debt actions are dealt with without the need for a full trial. If early judgment cannot be obtained and a full trial is necessary then a more detailed analysis than this Practice Note permits will be necessary.

4.1 A judgment in default

Court proceedings for debt recovery are by their nature for a fixed sum (together with interest and costs) and therefore practitioners do not need to concern themselves with judgments for damages to be assessed. Instead application can be made in both the High and County Court for a judgment in default of the defendant indicating that a particular matter is to be defended. Different procedures arise and different issues are involved in both the High and County Court.

4.2 Judgment in default in the High Court

Reference has already been made to the service of proceedings and the different ways this can be effected (see Chapter 3) and a defendant who wishes to defend a High Court writ must file at Court an 'Acknowledgment of service' within 14 days from the date of service of proceedings and as has been seen the date of service depends upon the mode of service effected.

4.2.1 The 'Acknowledgment of service' This is an important document. Notes for guidance of a defendant for its completion are attached to it and a defendant or his solicitor should heed those carefully. Any error or omission may bring the return of the form by the Court and enable the plaintiff to secure judgment in default. If a defendant wishes to defend the proceedings then the appropriate box should be ticked on the form and it should be returned to the District Registry from where proceedings were issued or alternatively to the Central Office of the Royal Courts of Justice. Alternatively a defendant may admit the debt is due and owing but ask for a stay of execution to prevent the plaintiff taking immediate enforcement action. If this is undertaken then a separate application supported by an affidavit must be made by the defendant to the Court and this must be made within 14 days from the date of acknowledgment. The affidavit will describe the defendant's means and put forward a proposal in this matter.

It is important that a plaintiff remembers that the effect of this is only to stay the execution process and it does not prevent a plaintiff obtaining a judgment, even though he cannot enforce that immediately. Providing the summons has been taken out, the stay continues until the hearing of that summons.

Obviously, if the defendant fails to take out the summons within the 14 day period after lodging the 'Acknowledgment of service', then execution can continue in the normal way.

4.2.2 Judgment in default of filing 'Acknowledgment of service' indicating notice of intention to defend Ord 13, r 1 (HC) If within the time prescribed by the rules, being 14 days from the date of service, the defendant does not file an 'Acknowledgment of service' indicating an intention to defend, then a judgment in default can be obtained by a plaintiff. This is obtained by completing a simple form of default judgment in duplicate (High Court Form 15). The form must incorporate the words 'No notice of intention to defend having been given'. These documents are then lodged at the office of the District Registry or the Central Office together with an Affidavit of Service duly sworn to prove that service of the writ has been effected. In addition technically the original writ should also be lodged although practice varies as to the necessity for this.

The form of Default Judgment would be duly completed to include the interest calculated up to the day of judgment and in addition the fixed costs. Details of the costs which are prescribed by Rules of Court are set out in Chapter 15.

4.2.3 Judgment in default of serving a defence Ord 19, r 2 (HC) In the High Court remember that if an 'Acknowledgment of Service' is filed indicating the intention to defend then a defendant must still serve a defence and this must be undertaken 28 days from the time prescribed for acknowledging service or of the time the statement of claim was served, whichever is the later. In the

28

vast majority of debt actions the statement of claim will be endorsed on the writ.

As has been stated already, in the vast majority of debt cases the statement of claim will be endorsed on the writ as it will be in a relatively straightforward form. Again a failure to serve a defence entitles a plaintiff to enter judgment and to complete the same form as previously described and attend at the Court Office with two copies. This form will incorporate the words 'No defence having been served'. The one difference from the procedure when an 'Acknowledgment of Service' has not been lodged is that the reverse of the form of judgment should have the endorsement, that is set out thereon, completed to confirm that the time for service of the defence has expired and no such defence has been served.

4.3   County Court procedure

4.3.1   Service   In a County Court (unlike the High Court) in the vast majority of cases, the court itself serves the proceedings which consist of a summons with a 'Particulars of Claim' attached and a form of 'Admission and Offer, Defence and Counterclaim' to be completed by the defendant (Form N9). The plaintiff will be told the date of service because the plaint note, which will be returned to him when proceedings have been issued, will be duly endorsed with that date of service and the defendant then has 14 days from that date in which to file his admission and offer, defence or counterclaim. If a plaintiff wishes to serve proceedings himself, it is open to him to inform the Court Office or similarly to inform the office if solicitors have indicated that service can be effected on them. In these cases an 'Affidavit of Service' or the solicitors' acknowledgment will be required to confirm the date of service.

4.3.2   Judgment in default, Ord 9 r 6 (CC)   If a defendant fails to file a defence or counterclaim or makes an unqualified admission on the appropriate form, then the plaintiff can immediately proceed to default judgment. The documents to be lodged or taken to the County Court Office are:

- The plaint note.
- The Request for Default Judgment Form duly completed (Form N14).
- Where service is by solicitor, an affidavit for proof of the date of service.

As in the High Court a correct calculation of interest should be undertaken to the date of judgment and fixed costs are also allowed as set out in Chapter 15.

The judgment date will also be entered upon the plaint note and entitle the plaintiff to pursue his remedies thereafter.

4.4   A defended debt action

4.4.1 Introduction If the defendant in a High Court action indicates an intention to defend or files a defence in the County Court a plaintiff has to make a decision as to whether or not he wishes to attempt to 'short circuit' the full trial procedure and apply for an earlier judgment under the summary judgment procedure available in both the High and County Courts. The nature of these procedures differs depending upon the Court as does the time when this action can be taken. However, it is an important remedy which should be seriously considered by plaintiffs who feel that a defendant may be seeking to delay payment without good reason or setting up a 'sham' or 'shadowy' defence. Before looking at the requirements in each court, it must be remembered that for the plaintiff to succeed completely through this procedure he would have to show that the defendant does not have any defence. The defendant would not have to show that his defence would succeed at a trial but merely that he has a *triable issue* and one which he should be entitled to promulgate at a full trial. If a plaintiff chooses to follow this route there is a risk that, if unsuccessful, then the time taken to have this issue tried may prejudice him, but, particularly in debt actions, it is a useful pre-emptive remedy which should be seriously considered.

4.4.2 The High Court (Ord 14 (HC)) The application is by summons supported by affidavit evidence which may include hearsay evidence. It is advisable to keep the affidavit evidence as short and concise as possible to add support for the plaintiff's argument that there is not a defence to the claim. A lengthy affidavit may well influence a Registrar to think that there must be a defence to the claim if the plaintiff has to explain his case in such terms.

In the High Court an application for summary judgment is usually taken out immediately after the 'Acknowledgment of Service' has been served by the defendant indicating that he wishes to defend the proceedings. There is however nothing to prevent such an application being taken out after a defence has been served, and in those circumstances the affidavit in support of the summons may well have to be slightly more detailed and indicate why the defence does not show a triable issue.

The final paragraph of any affidavit must depose to the fact that in the plaintiff's opinion, or that of his solicitor, there is no defence to the claim, and why that is so. The summons and affidavit must be served at least ten days before the return day and the defendant should then file his affidavit in reply indicating why he should be allowed to defend at least three days before the return day. Finally, the plaintiff does have an opportunity of filing rebuttal evidence by affidavit if necessary.

At the hearing which is before a Master or District Registrar there are several options open which are in essence:

- An immediate judgment for the plaintiff for the full sum claimed together with interest and fixed costs.
- A judgment for part of the s :n claimed together with interest and costs.
- An order that the defendant may have leave to defend the action but conditional upon paying the whole or part of the sum claimed by the plaintiff into Court.
- A dismissal of the summons on the ground that a defence has been shown.

In addition, the Master or District Registrar has discretion as to the cost Orders that he would make.

4.4.3 Summary judgment in the County Court (Ord 9, r 14 (CC)) The criteria for this application in the County Court are:

- that the plaintiff is pursuing a sum exceeding £500; and
- the defendant has delivered at the Court a document purporting to be a defence.

The plaintiff should take out an application supported by an affidavit verifying the facts on which the claim, or the part of it to which the application relates, is based and stating that, notwithstanding the document that has been delivered, there is no defence to the claim.

The 'Notice of the application', together with a copy of the affidavit in support, must be served on the defendant not less than seven days before the date fixed for the hearing (Ord 9, r 14(3) (CC)) and this hearing normally takes place on the same day as the pre-trial review (Ord 9, r 14(4) (CC)).

The Registrar has the same discretion as to the orders he can make as set out above for the High Court.

4.4.4 The defended debt action beyond summary judgment If a defendant successfully overcomes the summary

judgment application then the case proceeds, both in the High and County Court, in the normal manner as a defended action. Directions will be ordered and discovery of documents and inspection of those documents takes place. It may well be that at this stage the case becomes less of a debt recovery action and more of a defended piece of commercial litigation, (a subject which is outside the scope of this book). However, it is important to realise that by effective use of the Rules of Court and by continuing to keep on the attack a plaintiff's solicitor can still ensure that a successful recovery is undertaken either through the Courts or by a negotiated settlement.

For further information as to the procedures to be adopted beyond summary judgment see the Longman Practice Notes on *High Court Procedure* and *County Court*.

CHAPTER 5

ENFORCEMENT OF A JUDGMENT

5.1 Introduction

It is now assumed for the purposes of this book that a judgment has been obtained either through the defendant's default or through prompt and efficient use of the Rules of Court. Clearly however, the obtaining of the judgment may only be the beginning of the plaintiff's difficulties and the most important part of debt recovery work for a solicitor is the enforcing of that judgment. Each of the following chapters considers the major methods of enforcement which can be undertaken, both in the High and County Courts. It should be borne in mind however, that the initial instructions which were taken from the client will remain just as important at the enforcement stage as, hopefully, all relevant information for efficient enforcement will already be on the solicitor's file.

5.2 Choosing the correct method of enforcement

The major methods of enforcement of a judgment are as follows:

High Court:
- A writ of *Fieri Facias* (Sheriff's execution).
- Charging order.
- Garnishee order.
- Equitable execution (the appointment of a Receiver).
- Sequestration.
- Bankruptcy and corporate winding up.

County Court:
- Warrant of execution.
- Charging order.
- Garnishee order.
- Attachment of earnings order.
- The appointment of a Receiver.
- Judgment summons.
- Bankruptcy and corporate winding up.

(In addition, in both the High and County Courts a procedure for the oral examination of the debtor exists.)

It will be noted from the above, that there is no equivalent power in the High Court to the County Court's powers to make an Attachment of Earnings Order or to issue a Judgment Summons (except in family cases). The County Court has no power equivalent to the writ of sequestration.

It is too easy following the obtaining of a judgment to think that the difficult work has been done and simply to instruct the sheriff to attend to seize goods (in the High Court) or the bailiff to attend (in the County Court). Unfortunately, if these steps are undertaken without a consideration of all the circumstances of the debtor, then the client may not be best protected and it may simply be a case of further fees being incurred without appropriate recovery.

It is useful therefore to take stock of the situation and to consider each of the major methods of enforcement, to decide which method is likely to be the most successful for the particular circumstances of the case.

5.3   High Court or County Court enforcement?

It is often forgotten by practitioners that although a debt may have been incurred in the County Court it is possible in certain circumstances to enforce through the High Court. In addition, any High Court judgment or order for any sum may be enforced through a County Court (County Courts Act 1984, s 105) although it is difficult to envisage circumstances in which this would be appropriate.

The power to transfer any County Court judgment or order to the High Court is set out in the County Courts Act 1984, s 106 and the procedural requirements are set out in Ord 25, r 13 (CC).

The following circumstances and procedural requirements should be noted:

- there must be a judgment or order for the payment of a sum of money that has been given in the County Court; and
- the amount involved must be greater than £2,000. This is the current level specified by the Transfer of County Court Judgments (Specified Amount) Order of 1984 (Statutory Instrument 1984 No 1141).

If these criteria apply then the judgment may be enforced as if it were a High Court judgment and this has the considerable advantage that interest continues to run after judgment (unlike in the County Court). It will carry interest from the date of the transfer.

5.3.1   Procedure for enforcement in the High Court of County Court judgments   This procedure is set out in Ord 25, r 13 (CC) and also by a Practice Direction laid down by the Senior Master of the Queen's Bench Division and reported in [1988] 3 All ER 1084 as amended by a subsequent Practice Direction reported in [1990] 1 All ER 800.

The procedure is as follows:

- A request is made to the proper officer of the Court for a Certificate of Judgment.
- The certificate must state that it is granted 'for the purpose of enforcing the judgment (or order) in the High Court'.
- The certificate is signed by the Proper Officer.

Thereafter the judgment is treated as a High Court judgment and for all major forms of execution reference should be made in the documentation to the fact that the judgment has been transferred.

Upon transfer, of course, the judgment can be enforced with the generally more speedy methods of enforcement in the High Court.

5.4   Immediate enforcement or oral examination?

If full information is not known about the debtor, then many practitioners would advise that an oral examination of the debtor takes place before the Court. This is, in essence, a procedure whereby the debtor is examined on oath as to his means, assets and liabilities and a sworn document is produced which, hopefully, will produce more information for the plaintiff to be able to enforce his judgment more efficiently.

The disadvantage is that this procedure can be a slow and cumbersome one. Many debtors do not attend upon the first hearing, and only on the second or third hearing, when the threat of a committal to prison for contempt of Court is unleashed, is any information brought to the creditor's attention.

This procedure could therefore take several months, and indeed may well be a costly one, both in money and in chances of recovery of the debt for the creditor.

If the solicitor and client have worked together closely, then the information that an oral examination would reveal should, at least in part, be readily available.

For this reason, due consideration of all the facts of the case should be given before embarking on this procedure (a more detailed analysis is set out in Chapter 6). The relevant provisions are Ord 48, r 1 (HC) and Ord 25, r 3 (CC).

5.5 Obtaining priority over other creditors

It is not unusual, of course, for several creditors to be chasing the same debtor (both corporate and individual).

In these situations careful consideration of tactics must be adopted to ensure the best possible result for the client. A discussion of these tactics prior to the commencement of a debt action has already been made (in Chapter 2), but certain steps should be repeated when a re-appraisal is made post-judgment.

5.5.1 Company searches If dealing with a corporate debtor an up-to-date company search to reveal whether or not a receiver or liquidator has been appointed could save time and expense (although not necessarily bring good news for the client). Alternatively, by telephoning the Companies Court (on 071 936 6329) information could be obtained as to the presentation of a winding-up petition. Even if information is revealed to this effect, the opportunity exists for the creditor to give a notice of intention to support the petition and it may also be possible to 'stand in the shoes' of the petitioning creditor if he or she is paid prior to the hearing of the petition.

5.5.2 Land charges searches These searches at the Land Charges Registry may reveal whether or not any bankruptcy or charging orders are pending or have been made against the individual, and also may reveal further information such as charges that the debtor has created himself and therefore the full names of the estate owners.

5.5.3 Search at the Land Registry Without the consent of the registered proprietor this is only possible if a Registrar has ordered the same pursuant to an application for a charging order. However, a search of the Public Index Map Register should at least reveal whether the property is registered land or not and also provide a title number. This is useful and necessary information prior to making the application for the charging order.

5.5.4 Working together If other creditors are in a similar position against a debtor and are considering enforcement, then there may be merit in agreeing to work together and reach an agreement about payment of any funds recovered between the relevant parties and the sharing of solicitors' costs. Although there may be a saving in costs through this method the disadvantages are, of course, that there will be other creditors who will be sharing the monies recovered.

5.5.5 Swift enforcement In all debt recovery matters swift action is required but if creditors are aware of others seeking to recover money from the same debtor then it is even more important that a prompt decision is undertaken and efficient enforcement undertaken. If it is known that property is owned (either by the debtor on his own or jointly with his spouse) then the speed of obtaining charging orders over the property could be the difference between recovering and not recovering for a client.

CHAPTER 6

THE ORAL EXAMINATION

6.1 Purpose of this procedure

Both the High Court and the County Court have power to order a judgment debtor to attend before the Court to be orally examined as to means, liabilities, assets and circumstances. This power exists not only with regard to an individual, but, if the judgment debtor is a company it enables an officer of the company to be orally examined on the company's behalf.

It is a procedure that is often utilised to enable a decision to be taken upon the correct method of enforcement, but, as has already been said, it could delay the efficient enforcement of a judgment.

Accordingly, a solicitor and his client must balance the advantage of probably obtaining more information against the disadvantage of the probable delays accompanying this procedure. Having said that, the fees are comparatively low and certainly less than would be paid for other enforcement processes. The practice varies from court to court and therefore it is advisable, if conducting an examination in a court outside a solicitor's normal practice, to enquire whether or not or a representative should attend to conduct the examination or whether it will be conducted by an officer of the Court with a copy of the form then supplied upon payment of photocopying charges. As long ago as the late nineteenth century the courts made it clear that this procedure was to be taken seriously by debtors and in *Costa Rica Republic* v *Strousberg* (1880) 16 Ch D 8 the court stated that the purpose of the procedure was 'not only to be an examination, but to be a cross-examination, and that of the severest kind'. Unfortunately, many doubt the applicability of that statement.

Suggested forms of questionnaire, which can then be adapted by solicitors to each individual case, can be prepared but should not be slavishly followed and should be adapted depending on what information is discovered about the debtor.

In addition the debtor should be asked to ensure that all relevant books, documents, accounts, evidence of liabilities, evidence of third party claims and hire purchase claims should be produced as required by the Court Order.

6.2   Procedure

6.2.1   High Court Ord 48, r 1 (HC)   The High Court procedure for an oral examination is in fact more cumbersome than the County Court procedure and requires an affidavit to be prepared. The procedure is as follows.

Apply *ex parte* by affidavit (follow Practice Form PF 98—Vol 2 Part 2 of the White Book). The Court fee is £17.00. Then lodge the affidavit in the Central Office or with the District Registry where the judgment was obtained, with a draft Order (Practice Form PF 99—Vol 2, Part 2 of the White Book).

Thereafter the order, having been sealed by the Court, should be sent by you to the most convenient court for the debtor, which is usually the local County Court, together with a request in letter form that the oral examination do take place there. This is so even if the judgment remains in the High Court (see Practice Direction [1986] 1 All ER 128).

The County Court will insert the date of the appointment thereon and thereafter the order will be returned to be served personally by the creditor, his solicitor or an appointed enquiry agent. Remember, when serving the order, that travelling expenses for the debtor to and from the Court must be paid or at least offered, even if refused.

Inevitably there is non-attendance on the first hearing and then an application is taken out to commit the debtor to prison, which again is served personally as a Notice of Motion.

As in most court actions, any costs to be awarded by the Master or Registrar are at the discretion of the court but these would normally be awarded if it can be shown that there was merit in the oral examination from the creditor's point of view.

6.2.2   County Court Procedure Ord 25, r 3 (CC)   This procedure is much to be preferred, being simpler in terms of enforcement and in terms of issue. Again, make an *ex parte* application to the Registrar of the court in which the debtor resides (there is no need for an affidavit). Form N 316 of the County Court Forms is utilised, a fee of £12.00 is payable and the plaint note produced. It is usually endorsed with a certificate for postal service in Form N219.

As from 1 April 1990 the application must certify the amount remaining due under the judgment (SI 1989/1838 r 28). Upon receipt of the relevant documents, the court will fix a date for the examination and serve the order which should be effected a reasonable time before the day appointed for the examination. There is no obligation to pay conduct money (as defined in Chapter 1) at this stage.

If the debtor fails to appear at the oral examination hearing, which is not unusual, an order in Form N 39 will be issued at the creditor's request requiring the debtor's attendance at an adjourned hearing and in default he could be imprisoned for contempt. The court is in effect taking committal proceedings against the debtor for failing to obey its original order.

The adjourned hearing documentation (Form N 39) must be served personally by either the court bailiff or the creditor, not less than five days before the adjourned hearing and conduct money may have to be paid here if the debtor makes a request of the creditor not less than four days before the hearing. A certificate must be filed by the creditor not more than four days before the hearing, certifying whether conduct money has been requested and, if so, paid.

The adjourned hearing technically takes place before a judge, although in most courts hearings are now dealt with by the proper officer who certifies whether the debtor has appeared and if not refers the matter back to a judge for the making of a committal order. The usual order will be that the debtor is committed for seven days to prison, suspended on his attendance at a further hearing specified in the order for his oral examination. If the debtor attends, the oral examination is conducted as originally intended.

As with most County Court matters the court in which the application is made will be the one for the district in which the debtor resides or carries on business and therefore the application must be made to that debtor's 'home court'. No County Court can order a debtor to attend before another County Court for examination. Therefore, if the judgment has not been obtained in the debtor's 'home court' the judgment must first be transferred to that court by a request in writing pursuant to Order 25 r 2 (CC).

6.3   Action following the oral examination

It is vital that immediate action is taken after the oral examination pursuant to the information supplied. If property owned by the debtor is revealed for the first time and it is clear that equity exists then proceed by way of a charging order (see Chapter 8). If details of a bank account are revealed which would appear to be in credit then proceed by way of garnishee proceedings (see Chapter 9).

Alternatively, it may be that this procedure itself promotes an offer from the defendant to pay by instalments or even to pay in full. If this is the case, then it is hoped that the solicitor will have anticipated this and taken instructions on what sum will be acceptable to his client and can either agree to the making of the instalment order at the time, or alternatively, not accept that and seek to obtain a higher order or proceed to alternative methods of enforcement.

It is, of course, only a County Court that has power to order judgment to be entered for payment by instalments, although it is not unusual for a High Court judgment to be paid by instalments because of a private arrangement between creditor and debtor, or alternatively for there to be an order on suspension of a writ of *fieri facias* for payment by instalments. The difference is that no High Court judge can sign a judgment for instalment payments. This fundamental difference should be remembered, both generally and in relation to oral examination instalment offers.

CHAPTER 7

EXECUTION AGAINST GOODS

7.1 General information

Execution against goods is the most commonly used method of enforcement in debt matters. In general terms it is execution by the seizing and sale of goods and chattels of the debtor. The procedure is undertaken by utilising a writ of *fieri facias* in the High Court (Ords 45, 46 and 47 (HC)) or by a warrant of execution in the County Court (Ord 26 (CC)).

Although the most common method of enforcement, it can often be costly and not necessarily the most cost effective.

The Report of the Review Body on Civil Justice (Command 394) considered debt recovery as part of its ambit. It reported that in 1986 there were two million County Court claims for specific amounts of money and two hundred thousand claims in the High Court. The main findings were that the average County Court bailiff handled twenty warrants of execution per day whereas a High Court sheriff handled eight warrants per day and although the Review Body indicated that the recovery rate was broadly the same, most practitioners would question this, feeling that using the sheriff is a more effective means of recovering money than using the County Court bailiff.

With these caveats then, it is advisable to ensure the creditor knows exactly the procedure that is being adopted and the risks that exist (especially with regard to third parties laying claim to the goods) before execution is attempted.

This chapter will therefore consider the procedure to be adopted both in the High and County Courts and the problems that arise with this form of enforcement.

7.2 Execution against goods in the High Court—writ of *fieri facias* (Ords 45–47 (HC))

7.2.1 Introduction This is a form of execution through the sheriff that is adopted for High Court judgments and indeed County Court judgments that are transferred to the High Court for enforcement (see Chapter 5). By this procedure the sheriff is authorised to attend and seize goods in his bailiwick to the value of the debt and interest and costs (including his costs) and sell the same at an auction. He undertakes this procedure through his officer.

Unlike the County Court bailiff who is a salaried employee of the Court, the sheriff's officer is employed privately and therefore the cost of utilising the sheriff can be greater than that of the County Court bailiff. In the County Court, once the fee for issue of the warrant of execution has been paid (and this is a maximum of £38) that will invariably be the final payment. In the High Court, payment will be based on the hourly rates of the sheriff's officers. For full details of the sheriff's fees see the Sheriffs' Fees (Amendment) Order 1971 (SI 1971 No 808).

7.2.2 Practice and procedure The creditor's solicitors should attend at the court in which the judgment was obtained with:

- the formal request for the issue of writ of *fieri facias* (called the *Praecipe*)—Practice Form No 86 White Book Volume 2 Part 2;
- an office copy of the judgment or order;
- two forms of the writ of *fieri facias* for sealing and filing, Form No 53, Appendix A, White Book, Volume 2, Part 2;
- the prescribed fee, currently £10.00, (see Chapter 15).

In addition, if more specialised and unusual execution is required, further procedural points must be followed and a detailed reading of 'The White Book' should be undertaken, in particular the Execution Table in Volume 2, Part 3C.

Remember also, the specialised procedure whereby a judgment is transferred from the County Court to the High Court and before that judgment can be executed by way of a writ of *fieri facias* there must also be produced at the Court Office the certificate of judgment duly sealed (see Chapter 5).

In due course one copy of the writ is sealed and returned to the creditor for enforcement purposes.

The writ of *fieri facias* must be executed by the sheriff in the bailiwick in which the defendant resides or carries on business.

Since it is often advantageous to issue proceedings in the home court of the plaintiff it will regularly be the case that execution is to take place in a different county and care should be taken to ensure that the correct sheriff and under-sheriff is instructed.

When the writ is sealed and returned, it is therefore sent to the correct sheriff, together with the lodgment fee of £2.30. It is also always advisable to forward in a covering letter as much information for the sheriff's officer as possible. If, as is hoped, information has been obtained concerning the debtor, then this should be placed in that letter.

Great care should be taken to ensure that the writ of *fieri facias* is completed correctly for if not, it will be returned by the Court or alternatively by the sheriff. The most important points to note are:

- It should be addressed to the sheriff (or London deputy) of the appropriate bailiwick. These were not generally affected by the reorganisation of counties under the Local Government Act 1972, but certain sheriffs have special designations and reference should be made to the Execution Table in the White Book, Volume 2, Part 3C.
- The Judgment should be recited.
- There should be a command to the sheriff to seize sufficient of the debtor's goods to cover the judgment debt and costs, plus the costs of execution, plus on-going interest pursuant to s 17 of the Judgments Act 1838 on the judgment debt and costs.
- There should be a command to the sheriff to make a report on the result of his execution.
- The date of issue must be endorsed thereon.
- The name and address of the solicitor and creditor must also be endorsed.
- The residence/place of business of the debtor together with all other relevant information to enable the sheriff to levy execution must also be endorsed.

7.2.3 Levying execution Armed with the relevant information from the creditor's solicitor and the writ, the sheriff's officer will attempt to levy execution by attending at the debtor's premises. He will then either seize the goods, or, and this is more common, take what is called 'walking possession' of them. This is an agreement whereby in consideration of the sheriff's officer not seizing the goods or leaving a man in close possession of them, the debtor agrees not to remove or otherwise deal with the goods. A short time is then allowed by the sheriff for the debtor to find the relevant sums of money, or alternatively to reach an arrangement with the creditor to prevent the goods being taken subsequently and sold at auction. If the debtor does dispose of the goods in contravention of the agreement he will be guilty of an offence for which he can be prosecuted.

7.2.4 Costs From 1 April 1990 fixed costs of £38 are generally allowed on issuing execution, but no costs are allowed in the case of a writ of *fieri facias* unless the judgment is for £600 or more, or the plaintiff has been awarded costs (see Chapter 15).

The creditor's solicitor should particularly note that as soon as the sheriff's officers attend, costs are being incurred by them and therefore if the debtor seeks to come to an arrangement with the creditor it is vital that all sheriff's costs and expenses are ascertained and taken into account in settlement. In addition, as this is a High Court judgment enforcement method, interest is ongoing on the debt and costs and must be calculated and added to the outstanding sum for the completion of the execution.

On a successful levy, sheriff's costs and those of his officer are calculated on a percentage basis of the value of the goods seized and sold. These costs called sheriff's poundage are 5 per cent on the first £100 and 2½ per cent thereafter (see Sheriffs' Fees (Amendment No 2) Order 1971 (SI 1971 No 808)).

Of further importance is the fact that if the levy is unsuccessful (for any one of a variety of reasons, for example the bankruptcy of the individual, the priority of other writs or the disappearance of the debtor) the creditor will still have to pay the sheriff and his officer and it is vital to warn the client about this.

7.3   Execution against goods in the County Court—a warrant of execution (Ord 26 (CC))

7.3.1 Introduction   The warrant of execution is the County Court equivalent to the writ of *fieri facias*. It is executed by the County Court bailiff who is a salaried employee of the Court. All County Court bailiffs are drastically overworked and hence the speed of response on warrants of execution can be extremely slow and, unfortunately, the success rate is comparatively low. There can be nothing more frustrating for a client than having paid the fee for issue of a warrant of execution and for him then to be told that either the defendant no longer resides at the address given, or there are no goods left upon which successful levy can be made.

7.3.2 Practice and procedure   Normally leave is not required unless special circumstances exist as set out in Ord 26, r 5 (CC). These special circumstances mirror the High Court requirements for leave to proceed. The creditor or his solicitor completes a form of request for the warrant. From April 1990 these forms have changed and care should be taken to ensure that the correct and most up to date form is used, ie form N 323. In addition the plaint note should be lodged and the appropriate fee paid, which is based on the amount for which the warrant is issued as every pound thereof or part produces a levy of 15p (the minimum fee is £5.00 and the maximum fee is £38.00 — see Chapter 15). On the new form N 323, the creditor or his solicitor must certify:

- the amount remaining due under the judgment;
- where the judgment is payable by instalments;
- that the whole or part of any instalment due remains unpaid; and
- the amount for which the warrant is to be issued. (SI 1989 No 1838)

It is vital that the Court is informed of any payments that are received direct after the request has been sent to the Court. These are new requirements from 1 April 1990.

Upon receipt of the above documents, the court will issue the warrant of execution and forward it to the bailiff in whose area the warrant is to be executed. There is space on the request form for the plaintiff or his solicitor to supply details which may assist the bailiff in respect of the execution. If this space is insufficient a separate letter should be written.

The execution then proceeds as per the High Court execution with the bailiff reporting the results to the creditor's solicitor or creditor direct. Unlike the High Court there is no sheriff's poundage payable and once the fee has been paid to the court for the issue that is the final fee. However, as has been stressed before, no interest is running on the judgment. These therefore are some of the factors to weigh up when considering a High Court or County Court action. As the sheriff's poundage (payable on a successful or withdrawn levy) is 5 per cent on the first £100 and 2.5 per cent thereafter, it could be a quite considerable sum, but the advantages of utilising the sheriff have been documented earlier.

7.3.3 Instalment order (Ord 26, r 1(2) (CC)) Where a court has made an order for payment of a sum of money by instalments (as is quite normal in the County Court) and default has been made in payment of such an instalment, a warrant of execution may be issued for the whole of the said sum of money and costs then remaining unpaid, or for part of the money due, providing that sum is not less than £50.00 or the amount of one monthly instalment, or four weekly instalments, whichever is the greater.

In order to take advantage of this procedure which could be useful to 'test the water' against a recalcitrant debtor the whole or part of an instalment which has already become due must remain unpaid and any warrant previously issued for part of the said sum of money and costs must have expired or been set aside or abandoned.

In this regard, there is now a new Ord 26, r 1(4) (CC). Under the old rule the Registrar could direct that notice of issue was given to the debtor but under the new rule the proper officer of the Court *must* send notice unless otherwise directed. The notice is a warning notice to the debtor that the warrant has been issued and that it shall not be levied until seven days thereafter. This means that a debtor has a normal seven day breathing space before the bailiff attends and is another factor that should be born in mind by those seeking to enforce.

7.3.4   County Courts banking process   There have been significant reductions in the County Court banking functions which have taken effect from 1 April 1990. It should be remembered however that the County Court will still handle payments under live warrants. However, because the Court will no longer have a record of payments, it will not be able to check that a defendant is in arrears when a request to issue or re-issue enforcement is received. This is of course particularly relevant for the issue or re-issue of a warrant of execution. Hence the new form N 323 throws the onus onto the plaintiff to complete the monetary details which were previously completed by the court.

Previously if a suspension of a warrant took place and then the defendant failed to pay pursuant to the suspension, it was possible to re-issue that warrant simply by a letter to the County Court. That is now not possible because the plaintiff has to certify the outstanding balance and therefore a new form (N 445) for the re-issue of a warrant of execution has been produced. Remember that payments under a suspended warrant or payments of a part-warrant, or after the bailiff has made an abortive return are made direct to the plaintiff.

7.4   Writ of delivery and warrant of delivery (Ord 45, r 4 (HC) and Ord 26, r 16 (CC))

Brief reference of these two enforcement procedures need only be made. They are similar to the writ of *fieri facias* and warrant of execution and relate to the enforcement of a judgment for the delivery or recovery of any goods, for example, goods pursuant to Consumer Credit Act cases, although the remedies laid down by the Consumer Credit Act 1974 and the Hire Purchase Act 1965 still remain.

The High Court follows a procedure similar to the issue of a writ of *fieri facias* and in the County Court although a different form is utilised (N 324—Request for a Warrant of Delivery) the procedure is still very much akin to the issue of a warrant of execution.

7.5 Particular practical problems with an execution against goods

7.5.1 Costs of execution The problems of the costs and the possible irrecoverable nature of the same have already been mentioned, particularly in relation to the High Court. In the County Court it may not be considered to be as great a problem but bear in mind that the only solicitor's costs allowed on the issue of a warrant of execution for more than £25.00 are £1.60, which hardly equates to the costs of undertaking that issue process.

7.5.2 Goods exempt from seizure Certain items are exempted from seizure, the most important being:

- wearing apparel;
- bedding and bedstead of debtor and his family (up to £100 in value);
- tools of the debtor's trade not exceeding £150.

For full details see the Protection from Execution (Prescribed Value) Order 1980 (SI No 26 1980).

7.5.3 Disputes as to ownership One of the most common problems when a sheriff or bailiff attends is for the debtor to claim that particular goods belong to a third party and are therefore not available for execution. Obviously if hire purchase or leasing documentation is presented and checked by the sheriff's officer or bailiff the matter can be clarified there and then, but it is often the case that ownership is claimed by the debtor's wife or another relative. There is a set procedure if a claim by a third party is made to goods seized. Notice is passed to the creditor or his solicitor and formal Interpleader Proceedings may well follow.

Once a formal claim is made then the creditor has seven days for a High Court writ or four days for a County Court warrant to admit or dispute the claim of the third party. This is a short time limit in which to take instructions and again indicates the need for the solicitor and his client to have worked closely together to be aware of the possible claims that may be made.

If the claim is not admitted within the time period set out, then an interpleader summons will be issued to resolve the issue as to ownership.

The procedure for interpleader proceedings is set out in Ord 17 (HC) and Ord 33 (CC) but it should be borne in mind that it can be expensive and time consuming. The legal costs involved may well be those not only of the solicitor's client, but also those of the third party and indeed those of the sheriff.

As both writs of *fieri facias* and warrants of execution are valid in the first instance for twelve months beginning with the date of issue, if the interpleader process is ongoing for a considerable period of time, care should be taken to ensure that the execution process is renewed to protect the creditor in priority to other subsequent execution creditors.

7.5.4 Insolvency One further common problem in execution is that the process is part underway when either the company goes into liquidation or the individual is adjudged bankrupt and the judgment creditor may well find himself thereafter dealing with the insolvency practitioner appointed. The position is that a judgment creditor may only retain the benefit of his execution if that execution has been completed before the commencement of an insolvency process and reference should be made to the relevant sections of the Insolvency Act 1986 (ss 183, 184 and 346). An execution is completed for a writ of *fieri facias* and warrant of execution when the goods and chattels that have been seized have been sold. In addition, where the amount of the execution exceeds £500 and goods are sold or money paid to avoid a sale, then the monies must be retained by the sheriff or the proper officer of the County Court for a 14 day period and if notice of insolvency is received during that period the monies must be paid to the insolvency practitioner. Again therefore caution must be advised with a client if execution is canvassed as an enforcement method and an individual or company is considered to be in difficulties.

It may be, however, that the execution route is chosen deliberately by an execution creditor to obtain a return indicating there are no goods upon which to levy, which in itself will then enable the creditor to pursue bankruptcy or insolvency remedies (see Chapter 12).

7.5.5 Competing creditors It is often the case that when an execution process is commenced it is discovered that other creditors are seeking to pursue a similar remedy. In this regard it is important to be clear upon the rules for competing writs or warrants of execution as there could be both High Court writs and County Court ones in existence.

The basic rules are:

- In the High Court priority is governed by the time the writ is received by the under-sheriff for execution.
- In the County Court, priority is governed by the time the request for issue is delivered to the Court.

If, therefore, writs are issued both out of the High Court and warrants of execution issued from a County Court, consideration must be made of the time of the delivery of the writ to the under-sheriff or the time at which the warrant is received by the Registrar.

7.5.6 Jurisdiction Pursuant to County Courts Act 1984, s 103 where a warrant of execution has been issued from a County Court against the goods of any person and the goods are out of the jurisdiction of that court, the Registrar of that court may send the warrant of execution to the Registrar of any other County Court within the jurisdiction of which the goods are, or are believed to be, with a warrant endorsed on it, or annexed to it, requiring execution of the original warrant.

7.5.7 Restoring priority If a writ or warrant is issued and then a judgment upon which it is based is later set aside but then restored on appeal, that writ or warrant returns to its original priority (*Bankers Trust Co v Galadari and Another* [1986] 3 All ER 794).

7.5.8 Other writs or warrants Where a situation arises when it is discovered that other writs or warrants are in existence, before continuing with the process consider whether or not an alternative enforcement method will be more beneficial. Bear in mind, in particular, that if bankruptcy or liquidation is commenced this may have the effect of depriving other creditors of the benefits of their execution, but by the same token bankruptcy or liquidation will be more expensive and there is no guarantee that it would promote the payment that is desired.

7.5.9 Withdrawal or suspension of execution process It is not unusual of course for the commencement of the execution process to result in attempts by the debtor to come to arrangements with the creditor for either payment by instalments or for other arrangements to be made. In the High Court if instalment payments are offered by the debtor, then the creditor should think very carefully about his future actions, because if he instructs the sheriff to withdraw then other creditors may be able to obtain priority by levying execution.

In addition the sheriff's officer will be able to submit his claim for poundage referred to earlier. The walking possession agreement to which reference has been made could therefore remain whilst appropriate arrangements are being made, but bear in mind that sheriff's costs will increase and any arrangement with the debtor will have to include these.

It is far more common for there to be applications for suspension undertaken in the County Court by the debtor. Thus do not be surprised if the issue of the warrant produces an application (completed by the debtor on Form N 245) to suspend the warrant. Notification will be given of the terms of the suspension applied for and a decision must be taken whether to accept those terms in order to save costs, or alternatively to attend at the date and time fixed by the County Court for the Registrar to make a decision on whether or not to allow the suspension.

7.6   The future

The rationale of the current reform process being undertaken by the Lord Chancellor is to transfer more work to the County Court. Debt claims are by far the largest part of the work of the civil courts and it is proposed (although not yet law) that all debt actions should be started in the County Court, although there will still be procedure to transfer County Court judgments above £2,000 to the High Court.

In addition, it is proposed that there should be reform of the law governing executions generally and the provisions that prevent certain items being seized under the execution process should be revised. Close attention will therefore have to be given to the provisions of these proposals as and when they come into force.

CHAPTER 8

CHARGING ORDERS

8.1 Background information

A charging order can be a very effective remedy for the enforcement of a judgment and is normally taken against land or an interest in land. However, there is nothing to prevent a charging order being obtained against securities, such as shares, or funds that are in Court. For the purposes of this Practice Note, however, the emphasis is on the charging order which is obtained over land. It is important to remember that the obtaining of the charge in itself will not immediately obtain the money which is the subject of the judgment. To obtain that money there must either be an application to enforce the sale of the property, or alternatively, a voluntary sale and, providing there is enough free equity, the judgment will then be satisfied. The effect of the charging order itself is to give the creditor security for the debt.

Both the High and County Courts have powers to make charging orders over land or an interest in land and the basic procedure is set out in Ord 50 (HC) and Ord 31 (CC) and in the Charging Orders Act 1979 (as amended).

It is fundamental when considering this area to be clear that a charge, be it over land or other security, creates an *equitable* charge for the judgment creditor over that security.

8.2 Jurisdiction

Although, as has been seen, it is possible to issue proceedings in the High Court for (within reason) any sum of money, when it comes to the enforcement of a judgment by way of a charging order, the County Court has exclusive jurisdiction for a judgment or order of less than £5,000. Indeed, even if the amount is over £5,000 then the County Court has concurrent jurisdiction with the High Court but it is suggested that the High Court would be the most effective court to utilise in those circumstances. This is because, as with all High Court enforcement, the judgment creditor is able to draft all orders rather than be dependent on the court. If there is a High

Court judgment under £5,000 then although enforcement may be taken through the County Court the judgment is still a High Court judgment.

As has been mentioned previously (in Chapter 5) a County Court judgment for a sum greater than £2,000 can be transferred to the High Court for enforcement. But in respect of enforcement by way of a charging order this procedure can only be undertaken where a sum greater than £5,000 is in issue.

The court does not have any jurisdiction to make a charging order when payments under an instalment order in the County Court are not in arrears (*Mercantile Credit Company Limited* v *Ellis* (1987) *The Times* 1 April). This is another reason for proceeding, if possible, in the High Court because the High Court has no power to make an instalment order.

One interesting variation in the County Court procedure is that, pursuant to Ord 31, r 1 (1)(CC), it is possible to apply for a charging order either in the County Court in which the judgment was obtained or to the Court for the district in which the debtor resides or carries on business, which would of course normally be the County Court for the district in which the property is situated.

8.3   Enforcement of charging orders in the High Court (Ord 50 (HC))

8.3.1   Procedure   In fact the procedure to be adopted for both High and County Court charging order applications is relatively similar. There are always two stages to any charging order application. The application *ex parte* for the Charging Order Nisi and thereafter the application for the Charging Order Absolute for which the debtor is given notice.

The requirements for the Charging Order Nisi in the High Court are an *ex parte* application by affidavit to the Practice Master or District Registrar as the case may be.

A fee of £17 is payable (see Chapter 15). Pursuant to Ord 50 (HC) an affidavit should disclose the following:

- Details of the judgment and the amount unpaid at the date of the application.
- The name and address of the judgment debtor and of any creditor of his whom the applicant can identify.
- Full identification of the asset which is to be charged.
- Proof by the deponent (which will be the solicitor or creditor) that the asset which is the subject of the application is owned beneficially by the judgment debtor, with details of the reason for that

belief and the affidavit must exhibit any documentary evidence to support the same.

As to belief of beneficial ownership, the creditor may be able to supply evidence from the Land Charges search or alternatively there may be letters from the debtor himself or an oral examination confirming the position. Alternatively a prior mortgagee may have confirmed the position. Each case must be judged on its own merits. In addition, if the property which is the subject of the application is registered land (and a Public Index Map search in Land Registry Form 96 will have confirmed this) then there should be a request in the affidavit for an order for the Land Registry to supply office copies of the entries on the register pursuant to s 112 of the Land Registration Act 1925 (as amended). (In this regard see as well Practice Direction 16A [1983] 1 All ER 352.)

This is a particularly useful procedure and an order would normally be made by the District Registrar to this effect and does enable the creditor to confirm ownership, see other charges and thereafter contact any prior mortgagees for information as to their debt.

Upon considering this evidence, it is hoped that the order is made and indeed a draft order should be submitted to the Court with enough copies for service. The form of order is Form No 75 in the White Book, Vol 2, Part 2, Appendix A. If a charging order is sought on stock or shares in more than one company then a separate order must be drawn up in respect of each company. It will then be for the judgment creditor to serve the debtor with the order and this should be done together with the affidavit which was sworn to obtain the order.

The order will have specified a return date for the hearing of the application for a Charging Order Absolute and the debtor would then have to attend to show cause why the order should not be made absolute.

Immediately after obtaining the Charging Order Nisi, it is incumbent on the creditor to register the charge before service (see 8.6.1).

Unless the court otherwise directs, the order must be served by the judgment creditor by ordinary service (that is by post or personally) at least seven days before the return day. Service is effected on the judgment debtor and, if the court so directs, on any other creditors of the judgment debtor and any other interested persons.

Thus it is always advisable to ensure that an affidavit of service is available at the hearing of the Charging Order Absolute to prevent any point being taken by the District Registrar that the order has not been served. The solicitor should also attend at the hearing of the charging order absolute with a draft order as the responsibility is on the creditor to draw up and serve that order.

The form of order is set out in Form No 76 in the White Book, Vol 2, Part 2, Appendix A. Although some solicitors take the view that once registration has been effected for the Charging Order Nisi that is sufficient, it is submitted (although extra costs are involved) that it is good practice to register both the Charging Order Nisi and the Charging Order Absolute. As this is a High Court judgment, interest is running at the normal judgment interest rate (currently 15 per cent).

Where a charging order is sought and made absolute, basic costs of £81.00 are added to the debt together with additional costs of £13.00 if an affidavit of service is required (see Chapter 15).

8.4   County court enforcement of charging orders (Ord 31 (CC))

8.4.1   Procedure   The procedure is very similar to that utilised in the High Court and set out in Ord 31 (CC). Again the procedure is undertaken initially *ex parte* by affidavit, with the details as set out in Ord 31, r 1(2) (CC) being included (these are similar to the High Court Affidavit).

In addition, as would often be the case, where it is a High Court judgment there must also be lodged (see Ord 25, r 11 (CC)):

- An office copy of the judgment.
- If a Writ of Execution has been issued—a copy of the sheriff's return.
- Further, the affidavit should verify the amount unpaid at the date of the application.

As is normal for all County Court enforcement applications, the plaint note should also be submitted. There are also fees of £12.00 to be paid (see Chapter 15). Upon receipt of the documentation the court will then place matters before the Registrar and if, as is hoped, the order is made, that order will be drawn by the court (to save time the judgment creditor may wish to draw the order). This will be in Form 86 in the Green Book. The courts no longer serve the order but it is for the judgment creditor to serve it by ordinary service (that is post or personally) and to ensure that an affidavit of service is lodged at the court before the Charging Order Absolute hearing.

At the further hearing the Registrar has a discretion either to make the order absolute, with or without modifications, or discharge it (Ord 31, r 2 (CC)) and he has a duty to consider not only the parties to the application but also other creditors as far as they are known. It is for this reason that the affidavit sworn on the *ex parte* application has to disclose the names of other creditors who may be affected by the application. Further copies of the Charging Order Nisi and the affidavit are to be served on such of these other creditors as the Registrar may direct (Ord 31, r 1(6) (CC)).

Particular problems associated with the position of other creditors are considered in section 8.6.

If the court makes the order absolute then it will be in Form N87 as set out in the Green Book. It will then be served by the court on the same persons as the Order Nisi.

8.4.2 Costs Fixed costs of £52.00 are allowed on a Charging Order Absolute in the County Court. If it is a High Court judgment being enforced in the County Court, interest still runs on the judgment debt, notwithstanding the making of the order in the County Court (*Board of Trade* v *Orakpo* (*Current Law* May 1989 para 328)).

8.5   Orders for sale following a charging order and the appointment of a receiver

8.5.1 Background It may be that the judgment creditor is content to sit back and rely on the security that the charging order (duly registered) affords. Alternatively, it may be known that a sale of the property is in progress and as, inevitably, a purchaser's solicitor will require the charge to be removed prior to purchasing, an appropriate undertaking from the debtor's solicitor to discharge the debt upon the sale may be sufficient.

However, in the absence of either a pending sale or satisfaction by other means, the creditor may wish to enforce his charging order, either by a sale or by the appointment of a receiver.

8.5.2 Enforcement of a charging order by sale (Ord 88 (HC) and Ord 31, r 4 (CC)) In the High Court the procedure is by an originating summons in the Chancery Division (even if the judgment was obtained, as is normally the case, in the Queen's Bench Division). The procedure is set out in Ord 88 (HC).

In the County Court, proceedings are commenced by an originating application together with an affidavit. The details of the affidavit contents are set out in Ord 31, r 4(1) (CC).

There is no reason why an application should not be made in the High Court for an order for sale, even though a County Court charging order has been obtained and it is suggested this may be a more effective way to enable the creditor to be in control of the proceedings.

One practical problem with an order for sale, which has exercised the Courts, has been where a charging order is held over one person's beneficial interest in co-owned land only (for example against one or two joint owners, who normally are husband and wife). It has now been confirmed that an order for sale can still be obtained pursuant to an application under s 30 of the Law of Property Act 1925 (see *Midland Bank plc v Pike* [1988] 2 All ER 434).

8.5.3   The appointment of a receiver (Ord 30 and 51 (HC) and Ord 32 (CC)) It is appropriate to consider this matter in this Chapter although it is a procedure that is rarely exercised. Reference is also made to this remedy in Chapter 11. It is not limited however, to the appointment pursuant to a charging order but in all cases in which it appears to the court to be just and convenient to appoint a receiver.

Given that other methods of protection are available, this power should need to be exercised on relatively few occasions. In particular, possibly, where there is fear that in the absence of protection some property may be dissipated. In this case the procedure can be used swiftly and an interim receiver appointed.

The court will ensure that the receiver has the necessary powers to obtain money for the creditor from the assets specified in the order.

In the High Court a summons is taken out before the Master or District Registrar, with an affidavit in support which will have to depose to the reasons why the order is being sought (Ord 51). The relevant forms are the summons for the appointment of a receiver (Form No 82 in the White Book, Vol 2, Part 2, Appendix A) and the order appointing the receiver (Form No 84 in the White Book Vol 2, Part 2, Appendix A).

In the County Court, the registrar has jurisdiction and again the application is made by notice of application with an affidavit in support.

If consideration of the appointment of a receiver is to be made to protect the proceeds of sale of land, then the costs of such an application must be considered and discussed with the creditor. A receiver is normally a solicitor or accountant and he will often not take office unless satisfied that the assets will be adequate to meet his remuneration, or alternatively that he has been given a complete indemnity by the judgment creditor. As other professional persons become involved the costs increase proportionately.

As stated above, do not only consider the appointment of a receiver in respect of the protection of proceeds of sale of land, but a receiver could also protect an interest that the debtor has in, for example:

- rents from a property, or
- income from a trust fund.

8.6 Practical problems concerning charging orders

8.6.1 Registration As stated above, an equitable charge created by a charging order needs to be protected by registration. It is submitted that this should be undertaken at both the Charging Order Nisi and the Charging Order Absolute stages.

A different procedure should be adopted depending on whether the charge relates to:

- unregistered land, or
- registered land.

(a) Unregistered Land A charging order is protected by registration at HM Land Registry of a writ or order affecting land pursuant to the Land Charges Act 1972, s 6. Form K4 is used and the cost is £1 per name registered.

If this is done, then if the land is subsequently disposed of, any person taking the land will be bound by the charging order unless he is able to take free from it through the priority period given by an official search certificate. Indeed if there is fear that the land will be disposed of prior to the registration of the charging order it is possible to apply for the registration of a pending action at the land registry. Form K3 is used and the cost is £1 per name registered.

Considerable problems have been caused when considering the registration of a beneficial interest rather than the legal estate itself. This situation could, of course, arise when the judgment is against one joint owner. In the case of *Perry* v *Phoenix Assurance Plc* [1988] 1 WLR 940 it was stated that a charging order for an interest under a trust for sale (rather than a legal estate) cannot be registered as a writ or order. Statutory registrations are sometimes accepted by the Land Charges Registry but technically are of no protection to the creditor. His remedy would be to pursue an order for sale pursuant to the Law of Property Act 1925, s 30.

In addition, in this circumstance, the other owner or owners should be notified of the charge and this notification may be sufficient protection for the creditor. All prior mortgagees and other chargees should also be notified.

(b) *Registered Land*   If the charge is against the whole legal estate then this is registered by way of a notice on the charges register. This is undertaken by completing Form A4, HM Land Registry for which a fee of £25 is payable.

If the charge relates solely to an interest under a trust for sale, registration is by way of a caution against dealings. There is a risk that the caution registration could be 'warned off' on the grounds that it does not relate to land and by analogy to *Perry* v *Phoenix Assurance Plc*. The registration of a caution is undertaken by completing Form 63 (combined with Form 14) HM Land Registry and the fee is £25.

As can be seen, therefore, a charging order against the interest of one joint owner of property is no guarantee to successful enforcement. In practice, however, nearly all purchasers of properties so charged would seek undertakings from the vendor's solicitor (that is the debtor's solicitor) that the charges were removed and it is hoped therefore that normally the problems that technically exist would be overcome.

8.6.2   The discretion of the court   The granting of a Charging Order Absolute is within the discretion of the court and it must consider not only the interests of the debtor and creditor but other creditors. Other interested persons in the application should be disclosed in the affidavit and copies of the Charging Order Nisi and affidavit in support served on them. Interested parties could be other creditors affected by the proposed charge or possibly another joint owner, for example, in a matrimonial situation, the other spouse.

If it is known that matrimonial difficulties exist then a judgment creditor could well be faced by an application by the spouse to intervene in the proceedings.

A number of recent cases have considered the priority of a spouse's claim in matrimonial proceedings as against a Charging Order Absolute and the results are conflicting (which only serves to highlight the discretion that is vested in the Court). For a statement of the principles, see *Harman* v *Glencross* [1986] 2 WLR 637.

8.6.3   Insolvency   The test of 'completion' of execution is applied in relation to insolvency of a debtor when a charging order has been applied for.

The relevant law is found in ss 183 and 346 of the Insolvency Act 1986 and the relevant date for completion of execution is when the Charging Order Nisi is made. If the judgment creditor is able, therefore, to hold security successfully against the insolvency practitioner acting in the bankruptcy or liquidation he should liaise carefully with him as to what he proposes to do in relation to the property as that practitioner has powers of sale prescribed by the Insolvency Act 1986.

8.7 Conclusion

It is only worth undertaking a charging order application if a creditor is satisfied that not only does the debtor have an interest in the property to be charged but also that there are not prior charges which remove the equity. There will be nothing more frustrating than to advise a creditor that he is protected by a charging order only to find that, once the building society or bank has been paid, the amount of equity that is passed on is insufficient to satisfy the creditor and other avenues of execution have been lost.

CHAPTER 9

GARNISHEE PROCEEDINGS

9.1 Background information

The relevant rules are to be found in Ord 49 (HC) and Ord 30 (CC).

The basis of this enforcement procedure is that if the debtor himself is owed debts then these debts can themselves be attached by the judgment creditor in order to obtain his money.

The basic procedure in both the High and County Courts is the same, but note that the minimum sum in respect of which a garnishee order may be made in the High Court is £50 whereas it is £25 in the County Court.

The most common situation is where it is known that the debtor's bank account is in credit and an application is therefore made to garnishee that bank account. This includes not only current but also deposit accounts and would also cover building societies and other like institutions.

It must be remembered however that no order can be made to reduce below £1 the amount standing in the name of the judgment debtor in a building society or credit union account.

Examples of other debts that can be attached are as follows:

- A debt due under a dishonoured or stopped cheque.
- Future instalments of a debt payable by instalments.
- Monies in the hands of the sheriff under an execution (providing that money is to be paid to an individual and not to the Court).
- Most salaries when due as a debt (subject to certain exceptions)

The following have been held to be debts not attachable:

- Dividends distributable amongst creditors in the hands of an official receiver.
- Salary accruing but not due.
- Unliquidated damages, amounts not yet ascertained.
- Fees due from a solicitor to counsel.
- Maintenance or lump sum payments.

These are not exhaustive lists and reference should be made to the notes in both the White Book and the Green Book pursuant to Ord 49 (HC) and Ord 30 (CC),

In both the High and County Court, application is made *ex parte* by filing an affidavit.

9.2 Practice and procedure in the High Court (Ord 49)

9.2.1 Garnishee Order Nisi and Absolute As with the charging order procedure there are two stages, namely the Garnishee Order Nisi and the Absolute. The Nisi is obtained *ex parte* and the affidavit must set out the following information:

- The name and last known address of the judgment debtor.
- Identify the judgment or order to be enforced and state the amount of such judgment or order and the amount remaining unpaid at the time of the application.
- Depose that, to the best of the information or belief of the deponent, the garnishee (giving name, address and details) is indebted to the judgment debtor.
- Where the garnishee is a deposit taking institution having more than one place of business, give the name and address of the branch at which the judgment debtor's account is believed to be held and the number of that account, or (if it be the case) state that all or part of the information is unknown to the defendant. The affidavit should be as set out in The Queen's Bench Masters' Practice Form No PF 100 (White Book, Vol 2, Part 2).

When dealing with a deposit taking institution having more than one place of business it is therefore good practice to serve the order not only at the head office but also at the branch office, or, if the exact branch office is unknown, at all those at which it is considered the account could be.

Ensure that when lodging the affidavit a draft order is also lodged with enough copies for service and when the order is made by the Master or District Registrar a return date will be entered thereon and service should then be effected on both the debtor and the garnishee.

The relevant form of Garnishee Order Nisi is in the White Book, Form no 72, Volume 2, Part 2, Appendix A.

The fee for applying for a garnishee order in the High Court is £17 (see Chapter 15). Of course the important person to serve is the garnishee and he must be served at least 15 days before the hearing and should be served personally and then an appropriate affidavit of service prepared in readiness for the fact that the garnishee may not attend.

As to the debtor there is no requirement to serve personally although the better view is that this should be undertaken. Service must be at least seven days before the appointment on the judgment debtor but his non-attendance at the hearing of the Garnishee Order Absolute application will not be fatal.

For obvious reasons the garnishee should be served first to prevent the debtor seeking to deal with any money prior to the garnishee having notice of the same.

If these requirements are complied with then this matter will proceed to the Garnishee Hearing Absolute where the garnishee could attend and seek to prevent the order being made. It is often the case that correspondence has taken place between the creditor and the garnishee prior to the hearing of the Order Absolute. The judgment creditor's solicitor should attend at the hearing with the order prepared (Forms no 73 and 74 in the White Book, Vol 2, Part 2, Appendix A, depending on whether the garnishee owes more or less than the judgment debt) and if the order is made it is then served on the garnishee.

9.2.2   Costs (see also Chapter 15)   Under Order 49 the garnishee is able to deduct for his costs (before payment to the applicant) the sum of £17. The judgment creditor's costs are calculated as follows:

- If the amount recovered is less than £140—one half of the amount recovered.
- If the sum recovered is not less than £140—£72.
- Where the garnishee fails to attend the hearing and an affidavit of service is required—an additional £13.

9.3   Practice and procedure in the County Court (Ord 30 (CC))

9.3.1   Garnishee Order Nisi and Absolute   The procedure as set out in Order 30 is in essence the same as set out for the High Court above. Ord 30, r 2 (CC) details the information that must be supplied in the affidavit which mirrors that of the High Court. The suggested form of affidavit is Form N349 in the County Court. As from 1 April 1990 the affidavit must certify the amount of money remaining due under the judgment and that the whole or part of any instalment due remains unpaid (SI 1989/1838 r 42).

As with normal County Court procedure the order would be drawn up by the court (although to save time it may be that the creditor would wish to lodge with the affidavit the draft order for the

Garnishee Order Nisi). There is a set fee payable of £12 to issue this application (see Chapter 15).

The prescribed form of order for the Garnishee Order Nisi is Form N84 in the Green Book (as substituted by the County Court (Forms) (Amendment) Rules 1983. For the Garnishee Order Absolute the forms are N85 and N85(1), the latter being where the garnishee owes less than the judgment debt.

Remember as well that if application is made in the County Court under a High Court judgment or order (which will of course rarely be the case) an office copy of the judgment or order and an affidavit verifying the amount due and a copy of the sheriff's return to the writ of execution (if any) must be filed as set out in Ord 25, r 11 (CC).

It is submitted that the best procedure would be for the creditor to serve the garnishee to ensure that proper service is effected. The 15 day period before the hearing applies, as in the High Court, and the debtor is served (by post) at least seven days after the garnishee and at least seven days before the return day (Ord 30, r 3 (CC)).

The order will of course have the return day set out thereon and at that hearing the garnishee can attend and the court will consider whether or not the order should be made absolute or otherwise. If there is a major dispute then the hearing of the Garnishee Order Absolute will in essence be a directions hearing and the determination of the dispute will take place at a later date.

There is a major change as from 1 April 1990. Previously, the garnishee could pay into court the sum due to the debtor (or a smaller sum if that covered the judgment debt) and that would stay proceedings. This procedure has now been changed to bring the County Court practice into line with the High Court. The garnishee is required to freeze any money at the Nisi stage and, if so ordered, to pay that to the plaintiff at the Absolute hearing. This is in line, of course, with the general curtailment of the County Court's banking functions. The change revokes Ord 30, r 4 (CC) and is effected by SI 1989/1838 r 43.

9.3.2 Costs (see Chapter 15) If the judgment creditor recovers less than £65 then he is allowed to recover in costs half the amount recovered. Where not less than £65 is recovered, £34 in costs are allowed.

9.4   Practical problems

9.4.1   The Court's discretion   In both the High and County Court (Ord 49, r 4 (HC) and Ord 30, r 7 (CC)) confirmation is given that the Court does have a discretion in deciding whether to make absolute a Garnishee Order Nisi. The Court must consider not only the judgment creditor, the judgment debtor and the garnishee but also the position of other creditors of the judgment debtor (see *Rainbow* v *Moorgate Properties Limited* [1975] 2 All ER 821).

The garnishee order is in essence an equitable remedy and it will not generally be granted if the effect is to prefer one creditor above another, if for example there is an insolvency situation.

Bear in mind as well that if the court decides not to make the order absolute in its discretion because of a liability dispute, then the judgment creditor could be involved in lengthy proceedings which again could act to his detriment and could mean that other creditors chosing other methods of enforcement may jump in ahead of him.

9.4.2   Particular rules for deposit taking institutions   Quite apart from a garnishee's right to deduct costs as set out earlier there are particular rules for deposit taking institutions who may deduct a further £30 for administrative expenses when complying with an order (Attachment of Debt Expenses Order 1983 (SI 1983 No 1621)). This makes it particularly important to ensure that the figures on the order are correct as to the amount to be paid over.

9.4.3   Crown debts   These generally cannot be attached (see Ord 77, r 16 (HC) and Ord 42, r 14 (CC)) but there is an exemption for the National Savings Bank which can be garnisheed in the same way as other bank accounts.

9.4.4   Insolvency   It has already been seen that in other types of enforcement a judgment creditor could come into conflict with an insolvency practitioner. The question to be asked is whether the execution is complete. For the purposes of a garnishee order the execution is complete when the creditor receives payment from the garnishee and this entitles him to retain the benefit of execution.

9.4.5   Striking at the right time   A garnishee order can be an effective enforcement procedure providing the creditor is reasonably certain of the information which may have perhaps been obtained through an oral examination when bank account details or building society account details are revealed. However, there is an element of risk involved and garnishee orders notoriously cause problems, particularly in the case of bank accounts.

It is particularly important to realise that an order will only be effective if money is in the account by way of a clear credit balance at the date of service of the order.

CHAPTER 10

ATTACHMENT OF EARNINGS

10.1 Background information

Somewhat unusually, this particular method of enforcement is only available through the County Court (with only very limited exceptions). The exceptions are:

- The High Court may make an attachment of earnings order to secure payments under a High Court maintenance order.
- The Magistrates' Court may make an attachment of earnings order to secure payments under a Magistrates' Court maintenance order; the payment of a fine, costs, compensation or the payment of a Legal Aid Contribution Order.

Subject to the above, the County Court has unlimited power and jurisdiction to deal with an attachment of earnings for any debt.

If the solicitor or his client is aware that the debtor is in employment then this could be an effective procedure whereby payments would be automatically deducted from the debtor's wages and paid to the court. Despite the changes in the County Court's banking function from 1 April 1990, the court will still receive payments under full attachment of earnings orders but in cases of maintenance only for suspended attachment of earnings orders.

It may be the case that an oral examination has already revealed employment details, enabling this procedure to be adopted. Remember however that there is a minimum sum below which an employee's wages are not allowed to fall, (called the Protected Earnings Rate) and therefore for employees on low wages this procedure may not be suitable.

The relevant law is to be found in the Attachment of Earnings Act 1971 and Ord 27 (CC). From 1 April 1990 there is a new Request for Attachment of Earnings Form (N 337) which, as with the other enforcement form alterations, contains the requirement by the plaintiff or his solicitor to certify the amount due and owing. This must not only be certified at the time of making the application but also when the hearing takes place.

10.2 Practice and procedure in the County Court (Ord 27 (CC))

In order to apply for an attachment of earnings order the plaintiff or his solicitor must complete and file at Court:

- Form N 337 (Request for an Attachment of Earnings Order) (Ord 27, r 4(1) (CC)) and duly certify the amount due and owing.
- The plaint note (always submitted for enforcement),
- The fee of 10p for every £1 or part, with a minimum of £5 and a maximum of £40 (not payable when an attachment of earnings order is made on the hearing of a judgment summons).

It is a wise step to search in the debtor's home court for existing attachment of earnings orders (see Chapter 2). Any person with a judgment can undertake this search. If an attachment of earnings order is found to exist then the creditor may wish to consider consolidation with an existing order (see section 10.4).

10.2.1 Procedure for non-County Court judgments As with other methods of enforcement there should always be lodged the office copy judgment and the affidavit verifying the amount due, and, for a High Court judgment where a writ of *fieri facias* has been issued, a copy of the sheriff's return (Ord 25, r 11 (CC)).

10.2.2 Venue (Ord 27, r 3 (CC)) The appropriate County Court is the one in which the debtor resides. This may of course not be the Court in which proceedings had been commenced and the judgment obtained and therefore a transfer should be undertaken (Ord 25, r 2 (CC)). A request in writing (a letter form is sufficient) is made to the Registrar of the Court in which the judgment or order was obtained stating the reasons for the appropriate transfer.

There is a safety procedure if the creditor does not know where the debtor resides, in that an application can be made to the court in which a judgment or order, sought to be enforced, was obtained (Ord 27, r 3(2) (CC)).

10.2.3 Procedure prior to hearing The court will normally serve the application (Form N 55) on the debtor, together with an appropriate form of reply (Form N 56). He has eight days to file a reply and a copy is then sent to the creditor. The debtor must receive the documentation at least 28 days before the hearing.

Most creditors are happy for the initial application to be dealt with in their absence (there is a space on Form N 337 to this effect

which should be deleted if there is a wish to attend). Obviously
dealing with matters in absence can save costs.

If Form N 56 is duly completed by the debtor then a proposed
order will be made by the registrar and sent to both parties (Form
N 57) and this will be served at least ten days before the return
date. Either may give notice to the other and to the court of objection
to its terms which must be done within five days of receipt of the
proposed order. In that case the hearing will take place on the date
fixed, otherwise the proposed order will be made into a full order.

10.2.4 Procedure at the hearing Obviously there could be a
number of different alternatives depending on whether the debtor
has completed the form of reply, whether he attends, or whether
there have been objections lodged. It is quite common for a debtor
not to have completed the form of reply but still to attend the
hearing, and in that case the normal procedure would be for the
form of reply to be completed before the hearing. The registrar does
have a discretion, if the debtor is being particularly difficult, to hear
him in Chambers. Often, there could be indications that the debt is
disputed and if this is the case the debtor will be advised to complete
Form N 56 and the attachment of earnings application will then be
adjourned for a short time for the application to set aside judgment
to be made. If difficulties still persist there is power to place a debtor
before a Judge and ultimately to have him committed to prison, but
this is very rarely undertaken (Ord 28, r 8 (CC)).

If the debtor does not attend or refuses to complete Form N 56,
the hearing is adjourned for service of Form N 58 which is an order
for the debtor's attendance at the adjourned hearing. The procedure
on an adjourned hearing is set out in a practice direction issued by
the Lord Chancellor and dated 2 September 1981. This application
must be served personally at least five days before the hearing date
and it will be undertaken normally by the court bailiff. On service,
he will give the debtor another opportunity to complete his statement of earnings (Form N 56). This may well then trigger the
process for the registrar to make an order without the attendance
of the parties.

A failure by the debtor to attend on the N 58 hearing means that
the matter is referred to the Judge for committal proceedings.

If the order is made it will be in Form N 60 (or Form N 64 where
it is suspended on payment by the debtor of specified instalments).
This order is sent to the debtor's employer.

10.2.5 Obtaining information from the employer By Ord 27,
r 6, at any stage of the proceedings a Form (N 338) can be sent to

any person appearing to have the debtor in his employment and this requires the employer to supply a statement of the debtor's earnings and anticipated earnings with such particulars as may be so specified.

Further, by Ord 27, r 15 (CC) and Attachment of Earnings Act 1971, s 14, the Court can order an employer to supply particulars of the debtor's earnings. The order is in Form N 61 and must be endorsed with a penal notice to a named individual of the employer ordering him or her to supply particulars of the debtor's earnings.

10.2.6 Amount of the order There are two phrases that are always utilised in attachment of earnings applications:

- Normal deduction rate (NDR).
- Protected earnings rate (PER).

The NDR is the amount which should be deducted regularly (normally weekly or monthly depending on how the debtor is normally paid) by the employer from a debtor's wages.

The PER is the minimum amount that the debtor must retain from earnings and is calculated by having regard to his resources and needs.

Registrars and courts are given tables of assistance in fixing the protected earnings rate although these are not binding. Practice can vary from court to court although in the past it has been clearly accepted that no debtor should go below subsistence level as defined by Income Support. With the onset of the Community Charge (or Poll Tax) it is submitted that changes will have to take place in the calculation of the protected earnings rate to take account of the new charge.

It should be noted as well, that an employer is allowed to charge 50p per deduction. For this reason many debtors would prefer monthly rather than weekly orders.

10.2.7 Costs (Ord 27, r 9 (CC)) (see Chapter 15) Costs are available for each attendance on the hearing of an application for an attachment of earnings order. The fixed costs sum is £5.50 plus court fee.

10.3 Administration of an attachment of earnings order

Obviously, if the information revealed through this procedure is that the debtor is self-employed or unemployed no attachment of earnings order can be made and the application will be dismissed. However, if an offer is made by the debtor then an instalment order for payment of the debt could be made but the creditor should be given an opportunity to be heard. Similarly a suspended attachment of earnings order could be made (see 10.5).

Subject to the above, if employment is continuing then the monies will be deducted with reference to the protected earnings rate, and the creditor will be paid, hopefully regularly. The order obviously will lapse if there are periods of unemployment.

One common problem is a change of employment. The previous employer has an obligation to notify the court of the termination. Unfortunately there is no positive obligation on a new employer to see whether or not an attachment of earnings order is in force. If, however, he learns of one he must notify the court and, hopefully, the order having been redirected to him will continue as before.

The Attachment of Earnings Act, 1971 does lay down offences if employers fail to carry out these requirements and indeed there is a similar obligation on a debtor to notify the Court of a change in employment.

However it has to be said in practice, that enforcement of such orders is not easy if a debtor is regularly changing employment. Under Order 27, r 16 (CC) the registrar has power to issue a summons pursuant to offences laid down in the Attachment of Earnings Act 1971 to order the defaulter to attend and show cause why there should not be punishment.

10.4   Consolidated attachment of earnings orders

Where there is already an attachment of earnings order and other applications are received then there is power to make consolidated orders (Ord 27, r 18–22 (CC) and Attachment of Earnings Act 1971, s 17). The procedure is laid out in Ord 27, r 19 (CC) and can be applied for by the debtor or by any creditor applying for an attachment of earnings order. It can only be made, however, with notice to all creditors. By Ord 27, r 20 (CC), if there is already an attachment of earnings order in force and a subsequent application is made and there is no application for a consolidated order, the court can make one of its own motion after all persons have had an opportunity to be heard.

Order 27, r 22 indicates how the court is to deal with payments under a consolidated attachment order and they are dealt with proportionately to the amounts payable. The court does have power to declare a dividend but this is rarely undertaken.

It should also be noted that if an administration order is made (see Chapter 11) then these are often supported, if the debtor is in employment, with an attachment of earnings order.

10.5 Suspended attachment of earnings orders

Through the power conferred by County Courts Act 1984, s 71(2) an attachment of earnings order can be suspended. If the debtor makes an offer to pay the debt by instalments then the making of an order suspended on the instalment terms may be to the creditor's advantage. The debtor may well not wish his employer to know that he has this judgment and may be prepared therefore to agree a higher instalment order than would otherwise have been the case. The threat of the attachment of earnings order being made if the instalments are not kept to, with possible employment consequences, may be a potent one for the debtor. County Court Form N 64 is utilised for a suspended attachment of earnings order. The debtor may well contact the creditor direct when completing Form N 56 with a request for a suspended order, and if both parties consent, this order could be made without attendance.

10.6 Practical problems

As stated above, although in theory the procedure should be an effective way of obtaining regular monies, the orders are not so successful in practice due in the main to:

- The fact that they do not apply to self-employed or unemployed persons.
- The problems caused by a debtor changing employment regularly or employment lapsing with no notification being made to the court.
- A failure of employers to co-operate with the court.

In addition if the individual subsequently becomes bankrupt, then the attachment of earnings order will not be effective. The court may indeed automatically discharge it in any event.

Despite the above, if an oral examination or information from the creditor reveals that the debtor has been employed with one particular employer for a considerable period of time and the prospects seem fair for that employment to continue then an attachment of earnings order should be an efficient way of proceeding. As the majority of orders are now dealt with without the attendance of creditors or their solicitors the costs should be kept to a minimum, even though the procedure can sometimes be somewhat slow in execution.

CHAPTER 11

SPECIALISED METHODS OF RECOVERY

11.1 Background information

Chapters 6 to 10 have dealt with the most common methods of enforcement of a judgment but there are others which are available and, in particular circumstances, can be of assistance. This chapter deals with those and also deals with the particular problems of satisfying judgments against a partnership and the Crown. Chapter 12 deals with enforcement of judgment by way of insolvency which has its own practice and procedure.

The more specialised methods available are as follows:

- Equitable execution.
- Sequestration.
- Judgment Summonses.
- Administration orders.
- Enforcement against the debtor's person-committal.

11.2 Equitable execution

It has already been seen in section 8.5.3 that after obtaining a charging order there can follow an application for a sale or the appointment of a receiver, and the phrase 'equitable execution' covers the appointment of that receiver. Historically it grew up, as did all equitable remedies, to cover gaps in the common law remedies and is now to be found in the Supreme Court Act 1981, s 37 and Ords 30 and 51 (HC) and the County Courts Act 1984, s 107 and Ord 32 (CC).

11.3 Sequestration

This is a specialised remedy that has been referred to in the media comparatively recently, most commonly when sequestrators attempt to deal with assets of trade unions involved in employment disputes.

In essence this is a remedy when a body or person is in contempt of court by disobeying an order. It is a remedy that is solely available in the High Court and the procedure is laid down in Ord 46, r 5 (HC).

The judgments or orders that may be in force by a writ of sequestration are:

- Those that require a person 'to do an act' within a specified time which can be extended if necessary.
- Those that require a person to abstain from 'doing an act'.

In both cases leave to proceed must be obtained because of the serious nature of this remedy. Leave to proceed is requested of a Judge by notice of motion and, if granted, a writ is then issued to the sequestrators to take possession of property or chattels of the person, corporation or body which is in contempt.

As can be deduced from the above, it would only be very rarely and in large claims that this procedure would be contemplated. A detailed study of Order 46, r 5 (HC) should be undertaken if this procedure is to be carried out.

Some protection is afforded to third parties who may wish to claim that goods subject to the sequestration are theirs and they have an opportunity to apply to the court for an enquiry to take place.

11.4   Judgment Summonses

Except for matrimonial cases these are only available in the County Court and again this is a little used remedy.

A judgment summons however can be a very useful remedy within its field. It exists to enforce:

- Maintenance arrears.
- Income and certain other specialised taxes.

The relevant law is found in Ord 28 (CC).

11.4.1   Practice and procedure   As with most County Court remedies it is enforced in the district in which the debtor resides or carries on business (Ord 28, r 1 (CC)).

The familiar procedure is undertaken for the obtaining of this judgment summons, namely the lodging of:

- A request (Form N 342).
- Plaint Note
- Fee—£12 (see Chapter 15).

There is an option to serve personally or by post but, for the avoidance of doubt, personal service should be effected and conduct money (as defined in Chapter 1) is optional.

Remember as well, that if a High Court judgment is to be enforced the normal rules for extra documentation (Ord 25, r 11 (CC)) apply.

The documents must be served not less than 14 days before the date fixed for the hearing and, as with an attachment of earnings order, if the debtor fails to appear the threat of committal hangs over him with further process to be served.

If the debtor appears, the normal order (if it seems he can pay) would be for a committal order suspended for a further time to enable payment to be made.

Alternatively the court could dismiss the judgment summons or make a fresh order or make an attachment of earnings order.

Therefore, although limited in scope, the threat of committal hanging over a debtor can be a very effective way of enforcing a judgment if the criteria are satisfied. Certainly in matrimonial cases it should be considered as a swift way to enforce maintenance arrears, and possibly a more effective way of proceeding than with other rather longer and more drawn out remedies.

With the changes from 1 April 1990 to the County Court's banking system, the court will now only receive payments under adjourned orders in the judgment summons procedure, whilst all other payments under enforcement or suspended enforcement will go direct to the plaintiffs.

11.5 An administration order (Ord 39 (CC))

This procedure requires a debtor to pay to all his creditors who are subject to the order an amount calculated in proportion to the amount owing to them and this is to be paid by instalments. Payment can be either in full or at an agreed number of pence in the pound.

Reference has already been made to this remedy in Chapter 10 concerning attachment of earnings orders. It is only available in the County Court and is one that is useful for debtors for if the creditor sees that the debtor is seeking to arrange an administration order then more often than not it will mean a long wait for payment. An order is clearly for the benefit of the debtor and therefore the onus is placed on him to ensure that it works properly and efficiently. In essence he will supply to the court a list of all his creditors and the amounts owed and the court will then consider all the creditors together and make a decision upon the debtor's proposals for payment.

11.5.1 Practice and procedure This is set out in Ord 39 (CC) and County Courts Act 1984, ss 112 to 117 (as amended).

They are made in the court for the district in which the debtor resides or carries on business.

Furthermore they can either be on the application of the debtor, or by the court on its own motion pursuant to an oral examination (Ord 39, r 2(2) (CC)) or, as has been seen, pursuant to an attachment of earnings application. Obviously there must be in existence a County Court judgment and, to bring this matter within the jurisdiction of the County Court, the total number of debts must not exceed that jurisdiction (currently £5,000).

If the debtor desires such an order then he lodges at court:

- Form N 92—Request for an Administration Order.
- The court fee of 5p for every £1 of the money paid into court in respect of debts due to creditors—see Chapter 15.

In addition if, on an application for an attachment of earnings order, the court considers that the debtor has other debts he shall be ordered, with a view to the making of an administration order, to furnish to the court a list of all his creditors and the amounts which he owes to them. This is undertaken on Form N 93 in the County Court.

In both cases the statements made are verified by sworn statements (Ord 39, r 3 (CC)). The court will then fix a date for the hearing of the application which must be not less than 14 days from the date of notice being given to the debtor and to each of his creditors.

A procedure exists for creditors to object to the including of any debt within the proposed administration order. This objection must be given not less than seven days before the day of the hearing and be lodged at court, together with reasons for the objection, and the documents sent to the debtor and the creditor whose debt is being objected to.

11.5.2 Procedure on hearing There are different outcomes depending on the attendance or non-attendance of the debtor.

(a) *Debtor fails to attend* If the debtor fails to attend then the application should either be struck out or adjourned. As has been said, the procedure is for the benefit of the debtor and it is true to say, because of the work involved, it is not popular with County Courts. Therefore it is essential that a debtor is present before any order is made. A failure by the debtor to comply after the event will also mean that the procedure is revoked.

(b) *Attendance of debtor (Ord 39, r 7 (CC))* At this hearing, creditors may be present and the registrar will check through the schedule of debts and deal with the same and check also that any amended amounts referred to in information supplied by creditors have been correctly entered. If further debt information comes to light then the hearing may be adjourned to give creditors an opportunity to be heard. If the registrar is satisfied, however, that the amended list still does not exceed the County Court limit of £5,000 he can proceed to make the order which is in Form N 94. Copies will be served on:

- The debtor.
- Every creditor from the list of debts.
- Any other creditor who has subsequently proved his debt.
- All Courts which to the knowledge of the registrar have a judgment against the debtor or proceedings pending for debts.

The order is posted in the office of the court for the district in which the debtor resides.

Power does exist by the County Courts Act 1984, s 112(6) for an order to provide for payment of the debts to such extent as appears practicable and registrars have been given guidance to avoid orders which would proceed for a number of years. It is felt that such orders would not give any incentive to the debtor in view of the length of time that would be taken to finalise the order.

11.5.3 Power to review the order (Ord 39, r 14 (CC)) To take account of future changes in a debtor's position there is power to review an administration order. A court which is satisfied that the debtor is unable to pay any instalment due can suspend the order, at such time and on such terms as it thinks fit, or vary the order. Although this would appear to be an advantageous procedure for the debtor, the sanction is that if he does not comply with any terms and is found to have acted unreasonably then the scheme can be revoked. Alternatively it can be converted to an attachment of earnings order which would of course give more security for the creditors.

11.5.4 The addition of later debts There is no difficulty with the addition of later debts and indeed, even if those later debts take the total outside the County Court limit, there is still the discretion in the procedure for the administration order to stand (County Courts Act 1984, s 112(5)).

The procedure for subsequent proof by creditor is set out in Ord 39, r 11 (CC) and the normal practice of giving notice to the debtor and other creditors for them to object to the addition is provided for. If no objection is given within a seven day period after notification, the debt is added, but subsequent creditors will rank for payment of a dividend after current creditors (County Courts Act 1984, s 113(d)).

11.5.5   Effect of an administration order   The advantage to the debtor is that no further enforcement procedure can be taken without leave of the court but the sanction is that if he fails to comply with the scheme it will be revoked.

From a creditor's point of view such orders are not very satisfactory because they are generally made against debtors who have no reasonable prospect of paying within a short period of time and, because County Court judgments do not carry interest, there is no protection for the creditor for the delay in receiving payment. However, in certain cases, given the impecuniosity of the debtor, the view may be taken that some money being received is better than none at all.

11.6   Execution against the debtor's person by committal

Reference need only be briefly made to the power to commit. It has already been seen that failure to comply with certain enforcement procedures (notably the oral examination, attachment of earnings and the judgment summons) can lead to the threat and ultimately the carrying out of a committal order. Such powers are very rarely exercised and the threat is often sufficient to ensure that the required step in the enforcement proceedings is carried out. From a practical point of view the advantage to a creditor of a committal warrant being exercised must be questioned if, as is often the case, the reason for debts being placed in the hands of a solicitor is to ensure that money is received.

For the sake of completeness however, reference should be made to Ord 45 (HC) and Ord 29 (CC). Both powers are similar and include the power to commit a director or officer if the party in contempt is a company.

If this procedure is to be followed then many cases have stressed that it must be followed exactly and a failure to do so will result in the order not being made. See *Williams* v *Fawcett* [1986] QB 604 and *Harmsworth* v *Harmsworth* [1987] 3 All ER 816.

In the High Court a notice of motion is issued by the party applying for the order whereas in the County Court the application is issued by the court itself.

11.7 Satisfaction of orders against a partner

The advantages of issuing proceedings against individual partners rather than a firm have already been stressed. Certain enforcement procedures can follow as of right whereas leave is required in other circumstances.

11.7.1 Enforcement of judgment or order against firm as of right (Ord 81, r 5 (HC) Ord 25, r 9 (CC)) A judgment or order against a firm may be enforced against:

- Any property of the firm.
- Any person who admitted in the action or matter that he/she was a partner or is adjudged to be a partner.
- Any person who was served individually as a partner and failed to appear in the proceedings.

11.7.2 Enforcing judgment against a firm with leave of the Court In circumstances other than the above, leave of the court is required and this includes execution against a member of the firm who was out of the jurisdiction at the date of issue of the writ of summons. In addition by Ord 81, r 6 (HC) and Ord 25, r 10 (CC) it is not possible to issue execution to enforce a judgment between a firm and its members without leave of the court.

Although leave to proceed will often be granted by the relevant court it is a further step in the proceedings which could be avoided if proceedings are issued against the partners personally at the outset.

However it may be the case, of course, that the partnership itself has assets and a judgment has been obtained against one partner. In this case pursuant to Ord 81, r 10 (HC) and Partnership Act 1890, s 23, a procedure exists for his interest to be charged.

11.8 Satisfaction of orders against the Crown

This is a specialised subject in itself and reference should be made to Ord 77 (HC) and Ord 42 (CC). The law is set out in The Crown Proceedings Act 1947. There is no prohibition against bringing a default action against the Crown but special rules exist if further information is requested by the Crown. Furthermore, no default judgment can be entered against the Crown except with leave of the Court and no application for summary judgment against the Crown can be made.

When it comes to enforcing a judgment none of the normal

methods are available and instead a certificate of judgment is obtained which is then served on the solicitor for the Crown.

Because of the specialised nature of these proceedings, if a solicitor is instructed to pursue a Crown body there is no substitute for analysing the relevant High Court and County Court rules and ensuring that the client knows of the peculiar nature of this procedure.

It is of course comparatively rare that this procedure is necessary in general debt recovery work.

The Green Book sets out the relevant addresses for service under The Crown Proceedings Act 1947 and, from a practical point of view, assistance may be gained from the Treasury Solicitors' Department, Queen Anne Chambers, 28 Broadway, Westminster, London, SW1. Telephone: 071 210 3000.

CHAPTER 12

INSOLVENCY

12.1 Introduction and sources of law

The Insolvency Act 1986 revolutionised the law relating to both personal and corporate insolvency and the use of insolvency proceedings in debt recovery is now well established. However, the courts have been quite clear that insolvency remedies should not be utilised as debt collecting tools except as a last resort. This also makes practical sense for it must be remembered that if insolvency proceedings are commenced then the creditor could find that he will only be recovering a small proportion of his debt (for quite an expensive outlay). The basic difference between the use of insolvency as a debt collection tool and more conventional debt recovery methods is that the creditor in a bankruptcy or liquidation situation will have to share any monies recovered with other creditors. Hence it may well be the case that only a small proportion of the debt is recovered.

However, the threat of bankruptcy or liquidation may well produce payment in full and a solicitor should always consider this particular remedy with his client.

There are also other advantages to be considered namely:

- VAT bad debt relief is automatically available in an insolvency situation and therefore this will ensure that at least some money is recovered. (It should be noted, however, that a comprehensive new scheme for relief from VAT on bad debts was announced on 20 March 1990 through the 1990 Budget. The first claims for relief under this scheme cannot be made until 1 April 1991. Full details of the new scheme will be available in the revised edition of the HM Customs and Excise leaflet 'Relief from VAT on Bad Debts' which will be available from local VAT offices before April 1991.)
- The appointment of a liquidator or a trustee in bankruptcy could enable other routes to be explored for the benefit of creditors. For example, the activities of the directors in a company can be investigated, possibly to the financial advantage of the creditors (more information on this is set out in section 12.5).

12.1.1 Sources of law The basic law is found in the Insolvency

Act 1986, which is divided into separate parts and those relevant to this practice note are:

- Part IV, which deals with the winding-up of companies.
- Part IX, which deals with the bankruptcy of individuals.

In addition there are a number of statutory instruments that have been issued pursuant to the Insolvency Act 1986, the most important being:

- Insolvency Rules 1986 (Statutory Instrument 1988 No 1925)
- The Insolvency (Amendment) Rules 1987 (Statutory Instrument 1987 No 1919)
- The Insolvent Partnerships Order 1986 (Statutory Instrument 1986 No 2142)
- Insolvent Companies (Disqualification of Unfit Directors) Proceedings Rules 1987 (Statutory Instrument 1987 No 2023)
- Insolvency Fees Order 1986 (Statutory Instrument 1986 No 2030).

There exists a special procedure for dealing with insolvent partnerships. Partnerships may be wound up as unlimited companies under Part V of the Insolvency Act 1986 and the individual partners may be made bankrupt under Part IX of the Insolvency Act 1986.

Finally, although reference will not be made in any detail to it in this book, the Company Directors Disqualification Act 1986 is the legislation which enables courts to disqualify those who have been directors of companies which have become insolvent from taking directorships subsequently.

Practice directions (PD) and practice notes (PN) are regularly published in this area of law and care should be taken to keep up to date with the publishing of such directions. These normally form amendments to the procedure to be followed pursuant to the Insolvency Act 1986 and deal with developing areas of law.

The most important are:

- Hearing of winding-up petitions in London (PD No 2/86).
- Insolvency: hearing of applications (PD No 3/86).
- Proof of continuing debt on hearing of bankruptcy petition (PN No 1/86).
- 'Old Bankruptcy Notices'—transitional provisions (PN No 2/86).
- Individual insolvency: hearing of applications (PD No 4/86).
- Individual insolvency: hearing of applications (PD No 5/88).
- Bankruptcy petitions—creditors (PN No 3/86) (1987) 1 WLR 81 as amended by PN No 2/87 [1987] 1 WLR 1424.
- Substituted service of statutory demands and petitions (PN No 4/86) [1987] 1 WLR 82.

- Proof of service of statutory demand (PN No 5/86) [1987] 1 All ER 606.
- Application to set aside statutory demand (PN No 1/87) [1987] 1 All ER 607.
- Statutory demands—service out of jurisdiction (PN No 1/88).

Practice directions are issued for the most part at the direction of the Vice-Chancellor and have a binding effect. Practice notes are not intended to be binding and are issued by the Chief Bankruptcy Registrar. The latter are mostly intended to cure omissions or misleading notes in the prescribed forms.

12.2   The statutory demand

12.2.1 Introduction The statutory demand is one of the methods by which a bankruptcy or liquidation is triggered and it is not even necessary for there to be a judgment of the court for this procedure to be utilised.

A number of forms have been prepared for insolvency work and these are readily available from law stationers. The forms are prescribed by the Insolvency Rules 1986 (SI No 1925) and set out as Schedule 4 to these Rules. For the purposes of the statutory demand the following forms should be utilised:

- Form 4.1 for the winding-up of a company.
- Form 6.1 for a liquidated sum payable immediately by an individual.
- Form 6.2 for a liquidated sum payable immediately by an individual following a judgment or order of the court.
- Form 6.3 for a debt payable by an individual at a future date.

It is absolutely vital that the correct forms are used and that they are filled in correctly.

Particular points to note are as follows:

- State the debtor and creditor and relevant addresses.
- Set out full details of the money due; how the debt has arisen and whether any interest has been claimed.
- Ensure the form is signed by an individual (if solicitors are drafting this document then the individual solicitor should sign rather than his firm).
- For bankruptcy cases state the court to which application should be made to set aside the statutory demand, which is the County Court for the insolvency district in which the debtor resided or carried on business for the last six months. In this regard it is

important to remember that not all County Courts have bankruptcy jurisdiction and reference should be made to the index of County Courts in the Green Book to make sure this section is completed correctly.

A failure to complete the forms fully and correctly, could mean that there is an application to set the statutory demand aside but the case of *Re A Debtor (No 1 of 1987)* [1989] 2 All ER 46 stated that if the debtor has not been misled or suffered injustice then even if the form has not been filled out correctly in every detail the proceedings should still be allowed to continue.

The recent case of *Cannon Screen Entertainment Ltd* v *Handmade Films (Distributors) Ltd* [1989] 5 BCC 207 indicated, however, that if there is a dispute concerning the sum of money due then it is not correct for the creditor to issue a statutory demand before a judgment has been obtained. The normal order will then be for the statutory demand to be set aside and for an order for costs to be made against the creditor.

12.2.2   The statutory demand and the individual debtor   To issue a statutory demand against an individual there must be a debt that is equal to or exceeds £750 (or alternatively, an aggregate amount of debts to this level).

Besides stating the appropriate court for applying to set aside the document (see 12.2.1 above), the document must also state that if there is to be an application to set aside then action must be taken within 18 days from the date of service.

Service of a statutory demand on an individual is, except for exceptional circumstances, to be effected personally. The exceptions are, in general terms; if the debtor is deliberately avoiding service in which case there is the option of postal service, insertion through a letter box, advertising in a newspaper, or applying to the court for an order for substituted service (see Practice Note (Bankruptcy: Substituted Service [1987] 1 WLR 81).

It is important to realise however that a registrar will be loath to make a bankruptcy order unless he is absolutely certain that all proceedings including the statutory demand, have come to the attention of the debtor.

12.2.3   The statutory demand and the corporate debtor   As for the individual debtor, a sum of more than £750 must be due and owing and the statutory demand must be served on the company at its registered office. It is not sufficient to post the statutory demand. It must be delivered personally and left at the registered office.

Unlike the individual debtor there is no court specified to which application should be made to set aside the statutory demand (and consequently no 18 day period). If the debtor does dispute the document then the appropriate course would be to apply to the Court for an injunction restraining the presentation of a winding-up petition.

12.3 Individual bankruptcy

12.3.1 Grounds for petitioning for bankruptcy Apart from the statutory demand ground (which has been set out in 12.2.2), a creditor can present a bankruptcy petition against an individual if £750 or more is due and owing and execution or other process issued in respect of the debt on a judgment or order of the Court has been returned unsatisfied in whole or in part. The normal situation therefore is that a writ of *fieri facias* has been returned without levy by the sheriff's officer, or a warrant of execution has been similarly returned by the County Court bailiff.

Obviously for the obtaining of a bankruptcy order pursuant to the failure of execution, a judgment or order must have been obtained, but this is not necessary if a petition has been based upon a statutory demand. It is sometimes the case that a statutory demand is served to test the response from the debtor before conventional debt proceedings are issued.

12.3.2 Practice and procedure Prescribed forms in the Insolvency Rules 1986 (Schedule 4) exist and for an individual these are as follows:

- Form 6.7; failure to comply with the statutory demand for a liquidated sum payable immediately.
- Form 6.8; failure to comply with a statutory demand for a liquidated sum payable at a future date.
- Form 6.9; execution on a judgment has been returned in whole or in part.
- Form 6.10; on default in connection with an individual voluntary arrangement (as defined in Insolvency Act 1986, Part VIII).

The original petition, together with one copy for service and one to be exhibited pursuant to the affidavit of service and a further one for the petitioning creditor's file, are prepared. The original petition is exhibited pursuant to an affidavit which verifies the facts of the Petition (Form 6.13; Insolvency Rules 1986, Sched 4). In addition, where the petition is based on a statutory demand, an affidavit of service exhibiting that statutory demand must be filed at court.

A deposit of £240 for the official receiver's fees is paid to the court, together with the issue fee which is currently £45 (see Chapter 15).

It is important that the petition document is completed correctly, and indeed issued in the correct court (which will be the insolvency district where the debtor has resided or carried on business for the greater part of the six months immediately preceeding the presentation of the petition). This will normally mean that proceedings are issued in the County Court, although if a debtor has resided or carried on business within the London insolvency district, then the High Court has jurisdiction.

A search should be done in the County Court or the High Court to see if a bankruptcy petition has been issued by another creditor. If this is discovered, then obviously a further petition should not be issued but contact made with the petitioning creditor's solicitors indicating that support will be given and if that creditor is paid then the petition should be taken on by the further creditor.

Unlike company winding-up petitions, bankruptcy petitions are not advertised.

12.3.3 The bankruptcy hearing Bankruptcy hearings take place before a registrar in chambers and it is always advisable to attend with a draft order (in triplicate). In addition, the registrar must be informed of any notification received from other creditors, who either wish to support or oppose the petition.

There are a variety of orders which can be made on the hearing of the petition. In general terms these are:

- The adjournment of the petition.
- The dismissal of the petition.
- Substitution of another creditor in place of the petitioning creditor.
- The withdrawal of the petition.
- The actual making of a bankruptcy order.

If a bankruptcy order is made then the official receiver is immediately informed and he will act, until a trustee in bankruptcy (who must be a licensed insolvency practitioner) is appointed.

The costs orders that can be made depend upon the outcome of the hearing, but if a bankruptcy order is made then the normal order would be for the petitioning creditor's costs to be taxed if not agreed and to be paid from the estate itself.

12.4 The corporate debtor

12.4.1 Grounds for liquidation As this Practice Note is concerned with actions of creditors, this section is concerned solely with a compulsory winding-up order. It should be remembered, however, that a company can place itself into voluntary liquidation, or alternatively, may find itself struck off the register at Companies House for failure to deal with statutory requirements. Before embarking therefore on any winding-up proceedings, an up-to-date company search should be obtained, not only to see whether other creditors have taken proceedings, but also to see whether other insolvency processes have taken place. These may include the appointment of an administrative receiver by an individual or institution (normally a bank) which holds a debenture or charge over the company's assets. The appointment of an administrative receiver does not prevent winding-up proceedings following, but it is a strong indication of the unlikelihood of assets being available to satisfy the debt.

The statutory demand as a ground for winding-up a company has been set out in 12.2.3. Apart from that, the following grounds exist to trigger the issue of a winding-up petition for a compulsory liquidation:

- The company is unable to pay its debts; or
- the court is of the opinion that it is just and equitable that the company should be wound-up;
- the company has by special resolution resolved that it be wound-up by the court;
- in addition there are certain technical grounds where a winding-up petition would not be commenced by a creditor but by the company itself.

For the purpose of a creditor, the most important ground is that the company is unable to pay its debts and this is set out in the Insolvency Act 1986, s 122(1)(f).

A company is deemed unable to pay its debts if:

- A statutory demand has been served, 21 days have elapsed and the debt remains unpaid.
- Execution has been returned unsatisfied in whole or in part.
- It is proved to the satisfaction of the court that the company is unable to pay its debts as and when they fall due.

The most common grounds are the statutory demand ground or the failure of a writ of execution. Remember that for the statutory demand the debt must be greater than £750. This limit is not, however, necessary to commence proceedings through unsatisfied execution.

12.4.2   Practice and procedure   The prescribed form of the petition is Form 4.2 (Insolvency Rules 1986, Sched 4) and the original petition must be exhibited pursuant to the affidavit verifying the petition, which is set out in prescribed Form 4.3 (Insolvency Rules 1986, Sched 4). In addition, a copy for service should be taken to the court, with a further copy to be exhibited pursuant to the affidavit of service. It is always sensible to have one additional copy to retain on the solicitor's file.

A deposit of £240 for the official receiver's fees must be paid, together with a fee of £40 to the court. The official receiver's deposit, as with individual bankruptcy, will be refunded if the petition is dismissed or withdrawn.

A winding-up petition can be commenced in either the High Court or (if the paid up share capital is £120,000 or less) in the County Court which has jurisdiction for the area where the registered office is situated. Not all County Courts however have winding-up jurisdiction and therefore reference should be made to the County Court index in the Green Book.

The petition itself must be served in accordance with Insolvency Rule 4.8 which provides that it should be served at the registered office in any of the following ways:

- handed to a person who acknowledges himself to be (or to the best of the server's knowledge, information and belief is) a director or other officer, or employee of the company or;
- it may be handed to a person who there and then acknowledges himself to be authorised to accept service on the company's behalf or;
- if no person is there, as set out above, it may be deposited at or about the registered office in such a way that it is likely to come to the notice of a person attending at the office.

There are also provisions, if service at the registered office is not practicable, to serve it at the company's last known principal place of business, or by delivering it to the secretary or some director, manager or principal officer. Personal service should be effected, although there are provisions as to substituted service if this is required.

A winding-up order is advertised in the *London Gazette* (prescribed Form 4.6, Insolvency Rules 1986, Sched 4), which must take place at least seven business days after service and at least seven business days before the hearing.

A certificate of compliance (Form 4.7, Insolvency Rules 1986, Sched 4) must be lodged at Court at least five days before the hearing of the petition.

12.4.3 The compulsory liquidation hearing This is heard by the registrar in open court. Other creditors may support and if appropriate be substituted as the petitioning creditor. The petitioner must prepare for the court a list of the names and addresses of all those who had notified him of their intention to appear and hand that list to the court on the day of the hearing.

At the hearing the Court may:

- Make a winding-up order.
- Dismiss a petition.
- Adjourn the hearing conditionally or unconditionally.
- Make an interim order.
- Make another order it thinks fit.

If negotiations are continuing then the petition may well be adjourned although the courts have indicated that these should only be for short periods.

Costs are at the discretion of the court, but if the order is made for winding-up they will be paid out of the estate.

The official receiver is immediately informed once a winding-up order is made and he will then administer the estate pending the calling of a meeting and the appointment of a liquidator who will be an insolvency practitioner.

12.5 Procedure after the insolvency

The official receiver who will act initially in both bankruptcies and liquidations will in most cases call a meeting of creditors and at that meeting a trustee in bankruptcy or liquidator will be appointed. If the creditor is not able to attend the meeting there are provisions for proxy votes to be submitted. As a matter of practice, however, creditors should be encouraged to attend meetings to ensure their views are known.

Once the insolvency practitioner is appointed as trustee in bankruptcy or liquidator, then he will investigate the affairs of the individual or company and the Insolvency Act 1986 gives him a number of powers to look at transactions which have taken place and in certain circumstances he may be able to recover funds for the benefit of creditors.

For a detailed analysis of his powers, reference should be made to the Longman Practice Note on *Insolvency* by Steven Frieze.

12.6   Other insolvency proceedings

Although outside the scope of this Practice Note, the Insolvency Act 1986 created a new set of insolvency procedures which in general terms were attempts to provide rescue operations for individuals or companies in financial trouble. These are:

- An individual voluntary arrangement (Part VIII of the Insolvency Act 1986).
- A company administration order (Part II of the Insolvency Act 1986).
- Receivership (Part III of the Insolvency Act 1986).
- Company voluntary arrangements (Part I of the Insolvency Act 1986).

In addition, under the Deeds of Arrangement Act 1914, deeds of arrangement still exist for individuals but these are rare.

If a creditor is notified of any of these specialised insolvency procedures, then legal advice should immediately be taken as to the consequences for monies that are owed.

CHAPTER 13

INJUNCTIONS AND THEIR USE IN DEBT RECOVERY

13.1 Background information

There is often a fear amongst creditors that a debtor will seek to hide or remove assets in such a way as to make a judgment unenforceable. The law recognises this as a problem and accordingly a series of remedies has been developed to help reduce this problem and to assist in debt recovery.

In the vast majority of debt actions these remedies will not be necessary, but if there is a genuine fear then they are there to be used. Such remedies are often called 'pre-emptive' because, as injunctions, they can be undertaken without notice to the other party (*ex-parte*).

The three particular pre-emptive remedies which are most commonly seen in debt recovery work are:

- A Mareva injunction
- An Anton Piller injunction
- A Writ *Ne Exeat Regno*

13.2 The Mareva injunction

The essence of this procedure is that the court can grant either before or after judgment an injunction against the debtor on an *ex parte* basis if it can be satisfied that there is a risk that the debtor's assets will either be removed from the jurisdiction of the court (that is from England and Wales) or be otherwise dissipated.

This particular remedy is continually developing and now has statutory authority as set out in the Supreme Court Act 1981, s 37(3).

When the procedure was originally developed it was really concerned with cases where there was some foreign element, (for example where the defendant had links with another country) but that requirement is no longer necessary.

However, because the nature of this remedy is to proceed without notice to the other party, the court must be satisfied that full disclosure is made by the applicant of all the relevant facts, so that it can judge the matter fairly.

The procedure to be adopted is as follows—apply *ex parte* to a Judge (who will hear the matter in chambers) with the following documents:

- A draft order (preferably in triplicate).
- An affidavit sworn by the plaintiff or on his behalf by someone with knowledge of the facts deposed to.
- If proceedings have not been issued, then the originating procedure (writ and statement of claim or County Court summons and particulars of claim) must also be lodged.
- The issue fee (if in the High Court) for the *ex parte* application to the Judge is £15 (in addition to the normal issue of process fee). There is no fee payable in the County Court apart from the fee for the issue of proceedings.

In particular circumstances if there is a great urgency then the Court may accept an undertaking from a solicitor to lodge the originating process. Probably the most important document is the affidavit and the requirement to full disclosure is enforced strongly by the Courts who have regularly recognised the draconian nature of the remedy. In *Brink's Mat Limited* v *Elcombe* [1988] 1 WLR 1350 the court stated that the duty of the applicant was to make 'a full and fair disclosure of all the material facts'. This is an objective test and the court will require proper enquiries to be made before the application is lodged.

Each case will depend on its own facts but if proper enquiries have not been made because of time constraints the court should be told of this.

Clearly the most important paragraph of the affidavit is the reasoning for the belief that assets will disappear from the jurisdiction.

Because this is an *ex parte* application, the court will require the plaintiff to give an undertaking in damages that if the defendant ultimately succeeds at trial or succeeds in setting aside the injunction the plaintiff will compensate him for any loss or costs caused by the injunction. In certain circumstances this could be quite a severe undertaking and no plaintiff should consider it lightly. The court may order the money to be paid into court and the plaintiff must always show that there is money to back up that undertaking.

If all the above steps have been successfully completed, then the defendant is served (personally). Because the order takes effect as soon as it is given, service of not only the order but also the other documents in support must be undertaken forthwith.

As the injunction is relevant not only to the defendant but also those who may hold assets on behalf of the defendant (for example a bank) those parties should also be served.

13.2.1 Procedure after the order If the order has been obtained (as is normally the case) on an *ex parte* basis it will last for a short period and the Court will fix a date when the defendant will have an opportunity to be heard.

For the plaintiff, it is vital to remember that he continues to be under an obligation to inform the court of any new developments, certainly whilst the proceedings remain on an *ex parte* basis. This is also particularly important for a solicitor who has a personal responsibility to ensure that proper disclosure is made. In the recent case of *Manor Electronics* v *Dickson (No 2), The Times*, 8 February 1990, the court held that if there is a serious breach of duty by a solicitor in this regard then he may be ordered to pay compensation to the defendant.

There has been considerable discussion through the courts as to when is the right time to apply to discharge an injunction if there has been non-disclosure. The courts have varied between the view that this should take place at an interlocutory hearing or at the trial and the best advice that can be given is that each case depends on its own facts. If the non-disclosure is very pertinent then application should be made by the defendant as soon as possible.

A further example of a draft order for a Mareva injunction is set out at Note 72/A18 in the White Book and further information can be obtained from the useful Guide to Commercial Court Practice issued at the end of the Summer Term 1986 with the approval of the Commercial Judges and of the Lord Chief Justice. It is set out in Appendix A to Order 72 in the White Book starting at paragraph 72/A1.

13.3   Anton Piller orders

This is an exceptional remedy and is used even less frequently than the Mareva injunction. The essence of the remedy is that it is very much like a search warrant and is obtained if there is concern that documents or other property which should be inspected may disappear.

By the order the plaintiff and his representatives can enter premises and search and seize documents or property.

In certain cases Mareva and Anton Piller orders are linked together.

There are a number of similarities with regard to the procedure for a Mareva injunction and the pertinent points are as follows:

- The order can be obtained at any time before or after the commencement of an action and both before or after judgment; the remedy is *ex parte* by its nature.
- An on notice hearing will follow the *ex parte* hearing when the defendant will have an opportunity to be heard.
- The plaintiff should attend with the draft order (in triplicate) and the full affidavit in support.
- In the High Court a court fee for the *ex parte* injunction of £15 is payable. There is no such fee payable in the County Court.
- The burden is on the plaintiff to show a real possibility that the defendant may destroy the material before the trial and the requirements of full disclosure exist as before.
- The normal undertaking in respect of damages must be given.

13.3.1   Additional requirements for an Anton Piller order   A normal order requires an undertaking from a plaintiff or his solicitor that the order and evidence will be served by the solicitor. Furthermore, the court would require an undertaking that the defendant be informed of the effect of the order and have the opportunity of taking legal advice.

Finally, and obviously, there is an undertaking to keep safe anything that is seized.

Because of the quite complex and specialised nature of the order, careful drafting is essential. It would be sensible to ensure that a penal notice is endorsed on the order, which would mean that if there is a failure to comply then the defendant would be in contempt of Court and liable to be imprisoned. For further information concerning the correct way to deal with the execution of an Anton Piller order reference should be made to the case of *Columbia Picture Industries Inc and Others* v *Robinson and Others* [1986] 3 All ER 338.

13.4   Writ *ne exeat regno*

This is a little used procedure but also extremely draconian. It prevents a debtor leaving the jurisdiction and is granted if it is shown that the absence of the debtor would materially prejudice the continuance of the action by the plaintiff. The onus is on the plaintiff if he applies for such a writ and it is certainly not something that is used in conventional debt recovery. It has however been linked to a Mareva injunction if there is fear that this action may be defeated by the defendant leaving the country.

In practice, with the problems of checking at airports, the plaintiff should consider obtaining an order for the surrender of the passport at the same time.

13.5   Practical tips on these remedies

In view of the rarity of these applications in debt recovery, it is important that the correct procedure is followed. Judges will not grant the injunctions without being satisfied with the evidence and hence a very full affidavit must be sworn. It is necessary to ensure that the client is made aware in writing of the consequences of the undertaking as to damages that would have to be given and also to ensure that all necessary enquiries are made before launching forth into this procedure. Having said that, if genuine fears exist as to dissipation then the use of these pre-emptive remedies shows the defendant that the creditor is serious about his intentions and throws the onus very much on the defendant to deal with monies that are owed. Thus the injunctive relief could result in a swifter recovery than would otherwise have been the case.

CHAPTER 14

DEBT RECOVERY FOR SOLICITORS

14.1 Background information

Solicitors, as in any other business organisation, must ensure that they undertake efficient systems of debt recovery. Much therefore of what has already been said with regard to debt prevention applies to solicitors. However, when it comes to collecting outstanding costs, there are specific rules that apply to solicitors. It is the purpose of this chapter to outline those because a failure to deal properly or effectively with the detailed rules that exist could be fatal for the enforcement of a bill of costs.

In this chapter it is important to distinguish at all times between the collection of:

* Contentious costs, and
* Non-contentious costs.

For the purposes of the collection of solicitor's costs, a contentious matter is defined as business done in or for the purposes of proceedings begun before a court or before an arbitrator appointed under the Arbitration Act 1950, other than non-contentious probate business (see Solicitors Act 1974, s 87). Thus, some litigation matters will still be classed as non-contentious business, if proceedings have not been issued.

The Guide to the Professional Conduct of Solicitors, published by the Law Society, sets out the principles and makes reference to the Solicitors Act 1974 and The Solicitors' Remuneration Order 1972 which governs this area. The latest edition is published in 1990 by the Law Society, 113 Chancery Lane, London, WC2A 1PL

In addition, the Law Society publishes the following helpful booklets:

* An Approach to Non-contentious Costs;
* Contentious Costs and Solicitors Act Taxations;

which are both available from the Law Society's Publications Shop, 227/228 The Strand, London, WC2R 1BA.

If any particular point does not appear to be covered by the available documentation, then an enquiry either orally or in writing to the Legal Practice Directorate of the Law Society, (which is currently based at 50 Chancery Lane, London, WC2A 1SX) should be of assistance.

14.2 Collection of non-contentious costs

Principle 10.17, set out in The Guide to the Professional Conduct of Solicitors, states that in a non-contentious matter a solicitor may not sue the clients until the expiration of one month from the delivery of the bill unless the solicitor has been given leave to do so on the grounds set out in Solicitors Act 1974, s 69. Further a solicitor must not sue or threaten to sue unless he has first informed the client in writing of his right to require a remuneration certificate and of his right to seek taxation of the bill.

This is an absolute rule and therefore if this rule has not been complied with, any judgment obtained against a client is unenforceable.

It is submitted that the best practice would be to always append this particular notice to the bill that is submitted to the client. In accordance with normal contractual principles, it should either be on the front of the bill, or, alternatively, if it is on the reverse a solicitor should ensure that a sufficient indication of the notice is given on the front.

Because of the different requirements of suing for non-contentious or contentious costs, it is considered to be bad practice, and misleading, to include a notice relating to non-contentious costs on bills relating to contentious work.

There is no set form of words which must be utilised, although an example of the Notice of Rights under the Solicitors' Remuneration Order 1972 and on taxation is set out in The Guide to the Professional Conduct of Solicitors (Appendix C7).

The points that must be set out are:

- That the application for a remuneration certificate should be made within one month of the receipt of the bill.
- That the Law Society will be considering whether or not the sum charged is fair and reasonable.
- In addition, or alternatively, that the client can apply to the court to have the bill taxed by an officer of the High Court.

In addition, in a non-contentious matter, a solicitor may charge interest on the whole or outstanding part of an unpaid bill with effect from one month after delivery of the bill, providing the notice referred to above has been given (Principle 8.19 from The Guide to the Professional Conduct of Solicitors and Solicitors' Remuneration

Order 1972, Article 5). It may be sensible to append this information also to the bill of costs that is submitted. The rate of interest that is applied is the same rate as judgment interest (currently 15 per cent), pursuant to the Judgment Debts (Rate of Interest) Order 1985 (SI 1985, No 437).

If proceedings are subsequently issued, then interest can be claimed either pursuant to s 35A of the Supreme Court Act 1981 for High Court proceedings or s 69 of the County Courts Act 1984 for County Court proceedings (see Chapter 3) or, it is submitted, pursuant to the Solicitors' Remuneration Order.

A solicitor's High Court judgment will carry interest in the same manner as any High Court judgment, at the rate of 15 per cent as set out above.

14.2.1   The remuneration certificate If a client requests a remuneration certificate, then set forms are available from the Law Society which require the solicitor to complete detailed information upon his bill and to submit his file of papers and to disclose his charging rates.

14.2.2   Taxation of a non-contentious bill Although this option exists for a client and is governed by ss 70 and 71 of the Solicitors Act 1974, it would not normally be requested because the costs would often be disproportionate to the disputed element of the bill. The normal rule is that if more than one-fifth of the amount of the bill is taxed off, then the solicitor shall pay the costs of taxation, but otherwise the party chargeable shall pay the costs.

14.3   Collection of contentious costs

Pursuant to principle 10.18 of The Guide to the Professional Conduct of Solicitors in a contentious matter under s 69 of the Solicitors Act 1974, the solicitor may not, without leave of the court, sue the client until the expiration of one month from the delivery of the bill, save in certain specified circumstances.

The definition of contentious matters for solicitors' costs has already been referred to. The first point to note is that the Solicitors' Remuneration Order 1972 has no application to costs for any contentious work and furthermore interest is not recoverable upon the costs of contentious business unless:

• a solicitor has expressly reserved the right to claim interest in the original retainer; or
• the client has later agreed, for a contractual consideration, to pay interest; or

- the solicitor has sued the client for the costs, and claimed and been awarded interest thereon.

It will of course normally be the case that interest will be claimed in the proceedings pursuant to s 35A of the Supreme Court Act 1981 or s 69 of the County Courts Act 1984.

Furthermore, unlike a non-contentious matter, the client does not have the right to require the file to be referred to the Law Society for the issue of a certificate as to the reasonableness of the costs and any reference to this in a contentious matter would be misleading.

The client does have the right to have the bill taxed by the court, although interestingly enough there is no obligation to notify the client of this right, although as a matter of practice, it is suggested it should be undertaken.

An application for taxation should be undertaken by the client within one month from the delivery of the bill, although the court can still order taxation if the reference is made outside the one month period. If, however, it is made after the expiration of 12 months from the delivery of the bill then no order shall be made except in special circumstances and, if an order is made, it may contain such terms with regard to the costs of the taxation as the court may think fit (see Solicitors Act 1974, s 70).

Whilst the taxation process is being undertaken, pursuant to the Solicitors Act 1974, no action shall be commenced on the bill and any action already commenced shall be stayed until the taxation is completed.

The costs of taxation will be dealt with in the same way as the costs of the taxation on a non-contentious matter namely, that if one-fifth of the amount of the bill is taxed off, the solicitor shall pay the costs, but otherwise the party chargeable shall pay the costs, unless special circumstances apply (Solicitors Act 1974, ss 70 and 71).

14.4 General points

Inevitably any reference for a remuneration certificate or for the taxation of a solicitor's bill of costs will mean that delays are undertaken in the payment to the solicitor for the work done. This is a situation that any firm of solicitors will wish to avoid. Thus, a full explanation from the outset of the methods of charging, (such information being confirmed in writing) would be of considerable assistance. More and more firms are now adopting standard written explanations of the methods of charging at the outset of the business relationship and these are proving useful. Each case must, however, be judged on its merits and obviously dangers exist in giving estimates or indeed quotations for costs. Estimates and quotations are more normally found in non-contentious matters, notably domestic conveyancing but should always be confirmed in writing and the final figure should not vary to any large degree from the estimate unless significant changes in circumstances have taken place, which changes should also have been confirmed in writing.

A more formal contentious business agreement or agreement for the transaction of non-contentious business can also be entered into at the outset of the solicitor/client relationship. If these are undertaken, then, again, they should be fully documented but solicitors are warned of the dangers of relying slavishly upon them, without considering the circumstances of the individual case.

14.4.1 Maintaining cash flow Interim billing on matters, say every three or six months, has considerable advantages from a cash flow point of view, but it should be noted that if this is a bill on account, it cannot be sued on under the Solicitors Act 1974 and the bill should state clearly that it is not a final bill. Just as the solicitor cannot sue upon it, nor can the client apply for the right to have the bill taxed. Obviously, if difficulties arise pursuant to an interim bill, then a final bill should be submitted to trigger the rights set out above.

14.4.2 The form of the final bill There is no requirement for a narrative bill, setting out all the work done as submitted, but to prevent later difficulties it is considered to be a matter of good practice as, of course, any bill must relate to work properly and correctly undertaken.

In a contentious matter then, pursuant to s 64 of the Solicitors Act 1974, a client can insist on an itemised bill, but there is no such provision in a non-contentious matter.

Clearly, however, the more information that is given, the less opportunity should exist for argument.

Additionally, it is an often forgotten fact that a solicitor is not entitled to sue upon any bill of costs unless that bill has been signed by a partner or the solicitor's firm involved or, by the solicitor if he is a sole practitioner. The signing should be either in his own name or in the name of the firm.

It is possible to have the bill accompanied by a letter which is so signed and which refers to the bill, but the best practice is clearly to ensure the bill itself is signed.

Furthermore, in relation to the bill, all disbursements should be set out separately, and if they have not been paid, described as such (Solicitors Act 1974, s 67).

CHAPTER 15

FEES AND COSTS

15.1 Introduction and sources of law

This Chapter sets out the most common fees and costs in debt recovery work but for full· details reference should be made in the High Court to the Table of Costs which is published at least annually. The current Table was approved on 10 August 1990 and is compiled from Appendix 3 to Ord 62 (HC) (as amended) of the Rules of the Supreme Court 1965 (as amended).

For fees (as opposed to costs) reference should be made to the Supreme Court Fees Order 1980 (SI 1980, No 821 (as amended)). This is set out in Vol 2 of the White Book. The latest amendments are set out in the Supreme Court Fees (Amendment) Order 1990 (SI 1990 No 1460 (L13)).

In the County Court, reference should be made to Appendix B to the County Court Rules 1981 (as amended) for the relevant scales of costs. Again these generally change annually and come into force on 1 April of each year. For County Court fees the relevant order is the County Court Fees Order 1982 (SI 1982, No 1706) (as amended).

15.2 Fees and costs in the High Court

There is only one set fee for the issue of originating process in the High Court namely—£70.

The fee for an interlocutory summons in the High Court (except where the Order is by consent)—£10. The fee for an *ex parte* application to a judge in chambers (for example for an Interlocutory Injunction)—£15.

The aforesaid Table of Costs sets out the costs to be endorsed on a writ which vary depending upon the amount claimed; whether or not more than one defendant is being pursued; whether substituted service is being undertaken and finally whether service out of the jurisdiction is ordered.

The same table also sets out the costs that can be claimed in entering judgment in default of a notice of intention to defend or of defence. These figures again vary depending upon the amount claimed, the method of service, the number of defendants and whether or not the process was effected within or outside the jurisdiction of England and Wales.

15.3   High Court enforcement fees and costs

Fee on issuing writ of *fieri facias*—	£10.00
Fee to be paid to sheriff for lodgment—	£2.30
Costs allowed on issuing execution—(but no costs allowed in case of a Writ of *Fieri Facias* unless judgment is for £600 or more or the plaintiff has been awarded costs) generally—	£38.00
Fee on issuing an oral examination in the High Court—	£17.00
Costs awarded—At the registrar's discretion	
Fee on issuing charging order Application—	£17.00
Costs allowed where a charging order is sought and made absolute—	
1 Basic costs—	£81.00
2 Additional costs where an Affidavit of Service is required—	£13.00
3 Fee on issuing garnishee proceedings—	£17.00
Costs allowed—	
(a) Garnishee's costs to be deducted by him from any due before payment to the applicant—	£17.00
(b) judgment creditors' costs	
If the amount recovered by the applicant from the garnishee is—	
(i) less than £140—	one half of the amount recovered
(ii) not less than £140—	£72.00
(iii) where garnishee fails to attend hearing and an affidavit of service is required—	£13.00

15.4 County Court fees and costs

Plaint fees—

(i) To issue a Summons for the recovery of a sum of money, where the sum claimed or the value of the goods does not exceed £300—	10p for every £1 or part thereof claimed. Minimum fee £7.00
(ii) Exceeding £300 but not exceeding £500—	£37.00
(iii) Exceeding £500—	£43.00

Solicitors' costs set out on the County Court summons vary depending upon the amount claimed and whether service is by the Court or solicitor, and are as follows as from 1 April 1990:

Claim	£25–£250	£250–£600	£600–£2000	Exceeding £2000
By Court	£22.50	£30.00	£50.50	£55.00
By solicitor	£25.25	£35.50	£56.00	£60.00

The fees available on entry of a judgment again vary depending upon the amount awarded and are as follows, as from 1 April 1990:

	£25–£600	£600.01–£3,000	Exceeding £3,000
By default	£8.00	£15.00	£16.50
On acceptance of admission and offer	£14.00	£29.50	£34.50
Admission filed no offer or no accepted disposal	£19.00	£37.50	£44.50
Ordinary summons with no admission defence or counterclaim	£28.00	£41.75	£52.00

	Exceeding £500 but not exceeding £3000	Exceeding £3000
Summary judgment Order 9, Rule 14	£65.00	£74.00

15.5   County Court fees and costs — enforcement of a judgment

Oral examination (Ord 25, r 3 and 4 (CC))— Fee on an application for an order for the attendance of a judgment debtor or other person—	£12.00
County Court costs awarded—	For all County Court scales the costs are at the Registrar's discretion to award between £3.50-£10.50 per half hour spent or part thereof plus the Court fee.
Fee on warrant of execution—	15p for every £1 or part thereof of the amount for which the warrant is issued. Minimum fee £5.00, maximum fee £38.00.
Costs allowed on the issue of a warrant of execution for sum exceeding £25—	£1.60
Fee on an application for a charging order on securities—	£12.00
Costs (if allowed) on making of a charging order—	£52.00
Fee on garnishee proceedings—	£12.00
Costs—	If the Judgment Creditor recovers less than £65—half the amount recovered

Where not less than £65 is recovered—	£34.00

Fee on an application for an attachment of earnings order (other than a consolidated attachment order) to secure payment of a judgment debt

10p for every £1 or part thereof claimed

fees payable (for each defendant against whom an order is sought)—

Minimum fee—	£5.00
Maximum fee—	£40.00
Costs allowed (together with Court fee)—	£5.50

Fee on an administration order—

5p for every £1 of the money paid into Court in respect of debts due to creditors

Fee on judgment summons—	£12.00

No costs are allowed to a judgment creditor on the hearing of a judgment summons unless a committal order is made or the sum in respect of which the summons was issued is paid before the hearing. Where costs are allowed the sum is—

£5.50

15.6   Fees on insolvency matters

Personal insolvency
(on creditors' petition)

official receiver's deposit—	£240.00
Court fee—	£45.00

(on debtor's petition)

official receiver's deposit)	£120.00
Court fee—	£15.00

(can be reduced or waived)

Corporate insolvency

Official receiver's deposit—	£240.00
Court fee—	£40.00